Christian Science and Its Discoverer

E. Mary Ramsay

THE CHRISTIAN SCIENCE PUBLISHING SOCIETY

Boston, Massachusetts, U.S.A.

PUBLISHER'S NOTE

Changes made in this edition were recommended by the Archives of The Mother Church and are based on material pertaining to the life of Mary Baker Eddy which was not available when the author wrote her manuscript.

ISBN 0-87510-108-9

Library of Congress Catalogue Card No. 35-18957

Printed in the United States of America

Christian Science and Its Discoverer

PREFACE

IT was in the year 1913, when I was Christian Science Committee on Publication for the East of Scotland, that I was approached by an Edinburgh publisher who was anxious to obtain a short volume on Christian Science for his series, "People's Books." This series included short treatises on religious and philosophical movements of the day, all written from within. As in the course of my work I had encountered a number of short books and pamphlets purporting to explain Christian Science which were incorrect and critical, I was inclined to comply with this request, but I undertook nothing till I had referred the matter to members of The Christian Science Board of Directors, in Boston, who encouraged me to proceed. As the European War broke out soon afterwards, the work was laid aside, and was not completed till 1922. By this time the series for which the book was intended had come to an end, and the firm of publishers had been amalgamated with another. A publisher, however, was found in Messrs. Heffer & Sons of Cambridge, England, and the book appeared in 1923, and has been through two editions. It was primarily intended for the British Isles, and has also had some circulation in South Africa and in other parts of the British Empire.

Christian Science and Its Discoverer

The present edition has been carefully revised with the aid of competent authorities, including the Editor of the Bureau of History and Records of The Mother Church, and is now issued by The Christian Science Publishing Society.

E. M. R.

Edinburgh, March, 1935

CHAPTER I

MARY MORSE BAKER was born at her father's farm in Bow, New Hampshire, on the 16th of July, 1821. The house, though built of wood in the American fashion, was a comfortable, commodious building, two storeys high. It was sheltered from the north wind by the farmsteading, and by a stretch of woodland which lay behind, while the front of the house looked eastward, across the pleasant, old-fashioned garden, down the long, sunny slopes which fall to the Merrimac — a larger Tay. The strath through which this noble river runs is wide, fertile and varied, with a line of far blue mountains showing against the clear sky. The winters of New Hampshire are severe, much colder than in Scotland, but far more sunshine.

The house in which Mary Baker was born was the property of her father, Mark, and he and his brother James were joint owners of the 500 acres of farm land which they and their sons cultivated. In "Retrospection and Introspection," Mary Baker Eddy* speaks of broad fields of bending grain, of orchards where apples, pears, peaches and cherries grew, and of the large flocks and herds which grazed in the rich green pastures when she was a girl. But

*Mrs. Eddy is the Discoverer and Founder of Christian Science.

[1]

with the passing of the years, the countryside around the farmhouse at Bow has changed, and now the rolling hills and valleys are covered with pine groves and poplar, scrub oak and fern.

At the time of Mrs. Eddy's birth, the family circle consisted of the father, mother, three boys — Samuel, Albert, and George Sullivan — and two girls — Abigail and Martha. Mr. Baker's mother also lived with them and took special charge of little Mary.

The Baker family had been settled in New England for seven generations, John Baker, the first of the family to emigrate from England, being mentioned as a freeman of Charlestown, Massachusetts, in the year 1634. His descendants married into other well-known New England families, and thus Mrs. Eddy's ancestors included Captain Lovewell, the hero of the Indian wars, whose father had held a commission in Cromwell's army. Mrs. Eddy's mother was the daughter of a much-respected New Hampshire man, Deacon Nathaniel Ambrose, of Pembroke, a pillar of the Congregational Church, while her father's mother, the grandmother who has been mentioned already, was of Scottish descent, the granddaughter of John McNeil, who came of an old Covenanting family.

Her grandmother's stories of Scotland, of the long struggle with England for national independence, of the wars waged by the Covenanters for religious freedom, made a profound impression on little Mary and imbued her with a love for Scotland, which she retained all her life. In 1902 she wrote, "A Church in Scotland is dear to my heart, — it brings to memory the golden days of childhood, when Scotch tales were told at the fireside of my home."

At the time when Mrs. Eddy was born, the memories of the American War of Independence were still fresh; everyone was deeply interested in politics, in religion, in education. The Bakers' friends and neighbours owned their own farms, which their fathers and grandfathers had reclaimed from the primeval forest; all over the country churches were being built, schools and colleges founded. Mark Baker played a leading part in the affairs of the countryside, for, in addition to being a successful farmer, he was a well-read man of considerable intellectual power. He was often called upon to decide quarrels and make out deeds; at one time he acted as justice of the peace, at another we hear of him taking the part of counsel in a lawsuit and winning the case, the counsel on the other side being Franklin Pierce, who later became President of the United States. For several years Mark Baker was a Chaplain in the New Hampshire State Militia.

In politics, Mr. Baker was a Democrat, which then meant that he was a believer in State and local liberty, as opposed to the extension of national power; in religion, a strong Calvinist, a leading member of the Congregational Church. He was a man of iron will, dignified manners, careful of the education of his children, permitting neither profanity nor slang in his household, but hospitable, generous and kind to the poor.

Mrs. Eddy's mother, Abigail Ambrose Baker, was a remarkable woman. She was well versed in all the household arts and crafts of the time, could bake and sew, weave and dye. She also found time for visiting the sick, and for helping the poor. She kept a hospitable house, was a reader, thinker and interesting talker, whose society was enjoyed by the clergy and other leading men of the neighbourhood. Intelligent, sympathetic, bright and serene, she was a tender and devoted mother.

From a very early age Mary's striking character and endowments showed themselves. She was a lovely little girl with chestnut curls, deepset blue eyes and a beautiful complexion. Throughout her life she retained the erect, graceful figure of her youth, the shapely hands and feet. As an elderly lady she possessed a beautiful, delicate complexion, even less common in the drier climate of America than in these misty islands, and she had very fine features.

The little girl was considered delicate from birth, and it was soon found that the noise and confinement of the country school which she and her sisters attended were telling on her health. Mr. Baker consulted the leading doctor of the district, and was advised to take the child from school. "Do not doctor your child, she has got too much brains for her body; keep her out of doors, keep her in exercise, and keep her away from school all you can, and do not give her much medicine."

Thus from an early age until fifteen years or upward, her education was continued at home. This, however, was very far from being a disadvantage to her. She was by nature a student, acquiring knowledge with unusual facility, as she tells us herself in her autobiography, "Retrospection and Introspection," and she had the great happiness of studying under the direction of her favourite brother, Albert, a brilliant young scholar.

When Mary was about eight years old, a strange incident occurred, which repeated itself again and again during the space of a year. The child would hear a voice calling her distinctly by name, three times, in an ascending scale. At first she thought the voice was her mother's, and promptly answered the call, but Mrs. Baker declared that she had not called her, and could not account for what Mary had heard. This happened frequently, till at last the little girl felt discouraged, and the mother perplexed and anxious. At last a day came when a girl cousin who was visiting the Bakers heard the call too, and, seeing that the child remained sitting instead of attending to the summons, rebuked her sharply and told her to go to her mother. Mary went, and when Mrs. Baker again denied having called her, told her that her cousin had heard the call too. That evening, before the child went to bed, her mother read to her from the story of Samuel, and told her if she heard the voice again to answer as Samuel had done: "Speak, Lord; for thy servant heareth." The call came again, but the little girl was afraid, and remained silent. Afterwards she was filled with remorse; she cried and asked God to forgive her for her disobedience, and when the call was once more heard, she answered as her mother had bidden her do. That was the last time she heard the voice; the call never came again.

One evening in the November of this same year, little Mary begged her mother to let her go out to comfort the pigs which she heard squealing in their stye. At first Mrs. Baker said "No," thinking it too cold outside, but the child persisted in her request, and Mrs. Baker at last consented, as she had come to see that when Mary was much set on doing something it was well to permit her to do it. So her mother pinned a warm shawl round the child and let her run out of the house into the farmyard. Here she climbed on to the wall of the pigstye and sang a lullaby to the pigs, who responded to her kind thought and settled down comfortably to sleep. This happened several times.

In the same way the little girl's kind heart was greatly disturbed whenever her brothers fell out with one another. She always acted the part of peacemaker, and was never satisfied till they had made up their dispute and were friends again.

When Mary was nine years old, Albert won his

father's permission to go to college. He entered Dartmouth College, taking his degree four years later. After his early death, a friend wrote of him: "Albert Baker was a young man of uncommon promise. Gifted with the highest order of intellectual powers, he trained and schooled them by intense and almost incessant study throughout his short life. He was fond of investigating abstruse and metaphysical principles, and he never forsook them until he had explored their every nook and corner, however hidden and remote" (Retrospection and Introspection, p. 7).

It was on the occasion of Albert's first return from college that a very striking interview took place between him and Mary. He began by asking her if she had been allowed to have her books again, and finding her profoundly moved, got her to speak out with greater freedom than ever before. She told him of her great love for him and admiration for him, "how she recognized his bravery because he had persisted in his determination to go to college; and his honor, because he had never cried out against the hardship of labor that went hand in hand with his studies" (The Life of Mary Baker Eddy by Sibyl Wilbur, p. 25). This was a remarkable declaration for a child to make; it showed a discernment and power of expressing thought very rare at so early an age. What followed was striking, too: "When I grow up I shall write a book; and I must be wise to do it. I must be as great a scholar as you or Mr.

Franklin Pierce. Already I have read Young's *Night Thoughts*, and I understand it" (*ibid.*, p. 26). Albert answered by telling her to study her grammar — Lindley Murray's English Grammar — and his Latin Grammar, and promised to teach her Latin when he came home in the summer.

It was not surprising that Mary's imagination should be fired to emulate the example of her favourite brother, but it certainly was remarkable that she should have had the perseverance and ability to go on with her studies when he was away, so that at the age of ten years she was as familiar with Lindley Murray's Grammar as with the Westminster Catechism, which she had repeated every Sunday since she was a small child.

Albert, on his part, was faithful to his promise, and during his college vacations he found time to read with his little sister Moral Science and Natural Philosophy, and to give her lessons in Latin, Greek and Hebrew, while all the time he continued to read hard for his degree and to take a share in the work of the farm.

Mary had admired the courage with which Albert had insisted on going to college. Three years later she was called upon to make her first stand for her religious convictions, in opposition to her high-minded and determined father. In "Retrospection and Introspection" (p. 31), Mrs. Eddy says: "From my very childhood I was impelled, by a hunger and thirst after divine things, — a desire for something higher and better than matter, and apart from it, — to seek diligently for the knowledge of God as the one great and ever-present relief from human woe." At twelve years of age Mary was familiar with her Bible. She studied it by herself, wrote prayers after the style of the Psalms, and prayed seven times a day. From her earliest years she had been accustomed to listen to the theological discussions in which her father and his clerical friends took part. They were all strong Calvinists, firm believers in the doctrine of predestination. The little girl was greatly troubled by this doctrine. She was very much attached to her brothers and sisters, and so far they had not been "converted." She did not wish to be saved if they were to be numbered among those who were doomed to perpetual banishment from God's presence.

Mark Baker was much alarmed at the child's heretical views, and, hoping to win her from them, drew terrible pictures of the judgment day and eternal damnation. Mary's distress of mind at last brought on a fever, and the agonized father drove at a gallop for the doctor, thinking he was to lose his little girl body and soul. The family physician ordered complete rest and quiet, and left Mary in her mother's charge. As Mrs. Baker bathed her little daughter's burning brow she spoke to her of the great love of God, and told her to turn to Him in prayer as she had been accustomed to do. It was Mary's first experience of

[9]

spiritual healing. She prayed, and the intimate sense of God's love flooding her consciousness banished the terrible fear from which she had been suffering, and the fever, which was the outward manifestation of this fear, disappeared at the same time. Long years were to intervene, however, before the scientific explanation of this experience would dawn on her thought.

As a candidate for membership Mary had to pass through the ordeal of appearing before a church meeting to answer the minister's questions on the subject of her faith. She declared in the presence of all that she could never unite with the church if it was essential that she should accept the doctrine of predestination. Her earnestness made a deep impression. Later, at the age of seventeen, she was admitted to membership in the Congregational Church in Tilton, New Hampshire. She remained a member of this denomination till after her discovery of Christian Science, and she always speaks of it in her writings with much affection and respect. "I love the orthodox church; and, in time, that church will love Christian Science" (Miscellaneous Writings, p. 111). But, though Mrs. Eddy retained all her life a very loving memory of the religious surroundings of her childhood — the daily Bible reading and family prayers, the beautiful lives led by these old-fashioned clergy and their flocks, their charity, honesty, faithfulness and courage — yet in "Miscellaneous Writings" she affirms that she can attribute her long years of suffering to the misinterpretation of the Bible in the religious teaching which she had received as a child.

In 1836, the Baker family moved from Bow to Sanbornton Bridge, now called Tilton. Mr. Baker sold his share in the family property, and bought a farm about a mile out of the town. His sons had chosen occupations other than farming; Samuel was in business in Boston as a builder and contractor; Albert was studying law in Franklin Pierce's office at Hillsborough, and George Sullivan had gone to Connecticut for his health. Mary now attended a private finishing school for boys and girls kept by Professor Dyer H. Sanborn, under whom she continued her course of studies. She also received instruction from Mr. Corser, the scholarly minister of the Congregational Church. He was often at the Bakers' house, and a very warm friendship sprang up between him and Mary. They had long talks together on deep subjects, and he formed a very high opinion of her abilities and character. "Bright, good, and pure, aye brilliant! I never before had a pupil with such depth and independence of thought. She has some great future, mark that. She is an intellectual and spiritual genius" (The Life of Mary Baker Eddy by Sibyl Wilbur, p. 33). He spoke these words to his son Bartlett.

In the Congregational Church Mary Baker became a Sunday School teacher; she was given charge of the infant class, and speedily became very popular with her small pupils, who loved her brightness, her sweet smile and winsome ways.

In *Munsey's Magazine* of April, 1911, there is an interesting article entitled "The girlhood of Mary Baker Eddy," in which are given six letters written by Mrs. Eddy at an early age. The first of these was written when she was fourteen years old, before the family had left Bow; the other five are dated from Sanbornton Bridge (Tilton).

Five of these letters were written to her third brother, George Sullivan, while he was in Connecticut. The letters are long, as was the custom in those days when paper was expensive, envelopes unknown, and the charge for the transmission of letters high, so that the dispatch of a letter was a matter of some importance. Mary's letters show considerable literary style, though there are plenty of spelling mistakes and little inaccuracies in them.

The picture which these letters present is a very pleasing one. We see Mary Baker as a most loving, admiring little sister, looking up to Sullivan, as she calls him — her elder by eight years — as if he were a paragon of wisdom. She misses him greatly; misses his friendly advice and counsel, and the "lively interest" he had ever taken in her welfare. In one letter she expresses the hope that after she has read the book he has sent her she may become "some what more civilized"; again she speaks of the advice he had given her in a letter, tells him it was received very kindly, and that she intends to follow it, "not merely because it was enjoined upon me by a Brother, but because I consider it as important, as you feel it to be for me." She finishes the letter with the words, "Write soon dear Brother and give me all the good advice you can for yours is the genuine growth of experience." In another letter she writes, "Since I left you I have made it a religious duty to obey you in *all things*." (Possibly this remark was partly made in jest!) She refers several times in these letters to her bad health. In the letter written when she was fourteen, she says that her health is improving slowly, and that she hopes by dieting and being careful to sometime regain it. In a letter written two years later, she says that she has been studying every leisure moment this winter, and will attend school next summer if she can possibly manage to do so, but her health is extremely poor. She says she has had a very bad cold, which she put down to the severe climate. Next year she still speaks (this was after a journey) of her ill-health. "You cannot know how *lame* and unwell I felt *yesterday*."

In spite of these trials, however, the letters are those of a very happy, natural girl, full of little jokes and friendly chaff. Time, she says, glides smoothly with them, except when they are obliged to ride in a wagon. Again, in another place, she refers to the bad condition of the roads. She tells of a journey by coach, and says it was a sky-rocket adventure; sometimes it seemed as if she were midway between heaven and earth, till her senses were restored by the shrill whistle of the driver, or by a better piece of road.

In another place she writes, "Father has been speculating of late, although it is an allusion that in a letter might be considered rather abrupt, to tell you he has swaped [*sic*] your favourite horse with Mr. Rogers." In the same letter she tells Sullivan about a "perfect complet gentleman" from Boston, reading medicine in town, whom she had met a number of times at parties last winter. He had invited her to go to the Shakers with him, but "my superiors thought it would be a profanation of the sabbathe," so she did not go.

In the course of the letters she speaks of the election to the United States Senate of Franklin Pierce, the future President. Albert Baker had been reading law with him for a year or two, and now succeeded him in the law office at Hillsborough. Mary also alludes to her sister Abigail's approaching wedding. Abigail married Alexander Tilton, the owner of the cloth mills at Sanbornton Bridge, one of the family in whose honour the place was renamed Tilton. George Sullivan Baker was taken into the business, and, after a little while, became his brother-in-law's partner in this very flourishing concern.

In the letter dated April 17, 1837, when Mary was sixteen years old, occurs the following sentence:

"Martha has been very ill since our return from Concord. I should think her in a confirmed consumption, if I would admit the idea." It is striking that even at that date a belief that thought could affect health was already presenting itself to her consciousness. It was about two years after this that a young doctor, a cousin of the Bakers, came to Concord. He had taken up homœopathy. The subject was at that time quite unknown in New Hampshire, and at first was viewed with much suspicion; Mr. Baker, indeed, feared that his young cousin was "getting crazy." Dr. Morrill, however, was very successful with his treatment, and cured several people whom the regular physicians had been unable to help, so, after a time, Mr. Baker entrusted Mary to his care, and her health improved. From this time she became interested in homœopathy, and began to study the subject.

As we have stated already, Mrs. Baker was a thoroughly competent housekeeper; she instructed her daughters in the domestic arts, and found in Mary a very apt pupil. In later years, after the discovery of Christian Science, when Mrs. Eddy was occupied in teaching, writing, lecturing, organizing, she would find time to entertain pupils and friends, providing a meal which she had herself cooked and arranged. At eighty-five years of age, with the affairs of a great world movement on her hands, she still took an intimate interest in matters domestic. Dr. Allan McLane Hamilton, in an interview with the *New York Times*, said of her: "Far from being a mere visionary," Mrs. Eddy "is an excellent housekeeper, taking the keenest interest in the disposition of all her affairs and belongings. . . . She is accustomed to give minute directions about all the details of her household. Her own daily life is run on a thoroughly systematized set of rules. At six o'clock she is up and attending to her household affairs. . . ."

Mary Baker also possessed the gift of knowing how to dress well. As a girl she was noted for her pretty, becoming clothes, and for the grace with which she wore them, and to the very last she knew what to wear and how to wear it.

In 1841, to the great grief of his family and a wide circle of friends, Albert Baker passed away, while still a member of the New Hampshire legislature and while a candidate for election to Congress. Two years later Mary Baker married her brother Samuel's friend, George Glover, a young New England man, who had established for himself a good business as a contractor and builder in Charleston, South Carolina, and to this city the young couple departed shortly before the Christmas of 1843.

CHAPTER II

THIS change of residence from New Hampshire to South Carolina brought Mrs. Glover face to face with the controversy about slavery, which later was to plunge the whole country into civil war. In 1619, twenty negro slaves were sold to the English colonists of Jamestown, Virginia, by a Dutch man-of-war, and before the close of the century the hard labour of the southern plantations was supplied by black slaves.

When it is borne in mind that the United States — without counting Alaska, which was only purchased from Russia in 1867 — extends from the latitude of Cornwall on its northern to that of Calcutta on its southern boundary, it will be readily seen that the differences of climate are immense. The southern states with their warm climate and fertile soil required little skill in husbandry. A few staple crops were grown over wide areas; the system of cultivation was simple and uniform, while hard work in so hot a climate was trying to men of the northern races. On the other hand, in the states of the North, although there was a great demand for labour, slave labour was unprofitable. The agriculturist of the North had to be a man of initiative, resource and energy, able to turn his hand to any job that presented itself. We have already seen in Mary Baker's father and brothers the kind of men who tilled the soil of New England. Thus it came about that before the American Revolution, slavery was prevalent in the southern colonies, but was uncommon and unpopular in the North.

The American Constitution came into force in 1789, and in 1793 Eli Whitney invented the saw-gin. The saw-gin is an instrument for separating the seeds from the fiber of the cotton plant, an operation which up to this time had been chiefly performed by hand. An immense impetus was given to the cotton industry by the appearance of the saw-gin. Cotton became the most important crop of the Southern States, and as it exhausts the soil on which it is grown, there was a constant call for fresh soil suitable for its cultivation, where slave labour might be employed.

As the years passed, the feeling against slavery grew in the North, and there was more and more opposition to the inclusion in the Union of new slavery states, but "the South" formed a political whole, long before the Northern States had become "the North," and thus acting in agreement possessed a political power out of proportion to its wealth and population. In this way the dominant Democratic party of the South, combining with the Democrats of the North, governed the country almost continuously from 1830 to 1860. Every attempt to stop the spread of slavery was met by the threat of secession.

It was in the year 1845 that the last slave states, Florida and Texas, entered the Union, so it will be seen that the supporters of slavery were in the very heyday of their power when Mary took up her abode with her young husband in Charleston, South Carolina. The impression made upon her was distressing in the extreme. Mr. Glover possessed slaves, and Mary and he had discussions on this subject. He took the view that if he was to succeed with his business in the South, he must be prepared to fall in to some extent with the prevailing customs; he also argued that by the laws of South Carolina it would be difficult to free his slaves absolutely. But what to him appeared a matter of expediency, to her was a question of principle. She could not remain silent; she spoke out fearlessly.

In the February following his marriage, Mr. Glover went on business to Wilmington, North Carolina, and he took Mary with him. At the end of four months, and before Mr. Glover was able to finish his business in that city, he was attacked by yellow fever. He was a Royal Arch Mason, and his brother Masons did all they could to help him. As Mrs. Glover was in delicate health, they refused to allow her to nurse her husband, but a distinguished physician was called in and every arrangement made for his comfort. She was told by the doctor that her husband was suffering from yellow fever in its worst form, and that there was no chance of his recovery. Mary was absolutely devoted to her husband, as he was to her, and she prayed without ceasing for him during nine days and nights, but at the end of that time he passed away. Though his wife's prayers had failed to restore him to health, the doctor declared that Mr. Glover's life had certainly been prolonged by them, that in the ordinary course of things he would have died on the seventh day of the illness.

During his last days on earth George Glover spoke constantly of his young wife, and when he knew that he was dying begged his brother Masons to take her home to the North. The members of St. John's Lodge, Wilmington, and business friends conveyed Mr. Glover's body to the Episcopal burying ground, and here the funeral service was performed by the masonic chaplain.

George Glover, often called Major Glover from a post which he had held at one time on a Governor's staff, was only thirty-two years of age when he passed away. During the years spent in the South he had acquired a large circle of friends, and after his death the greatest kindness was shown to his poor young widow. She was tenderly taken care of and entertained, and at the end of a month was escorted to New York by one of the Masons and handed over to the care of her brother George, who came from New Hampshire to meet her. In "Retrospection and Introspection" (p. 20), Mrs. Eddy says, "After returning to the paternal roof I lost all my husband's property, except what money I had brought with me." With her father's full approval, she had allowed her husband's slaves to go free.

The home party now consisted of Mr. and Mrs. Baker, George and Mary, and it was soon to be increased, for in September Mary's son was born, and was called after his father, George Washington. Mrs. Glover was far too ill to be able to attend to him, and accordingly he was handed over to the care of a Mrs. Morrison, whilst Mahala Sanborn, the blacksmith's daughter, came to nurse her. For a long time it seemed doubtful if she would recover. It is touching to read of the devotion of Mr. Baker, sitting for hours by his daughter's bed and rocking her gently in his arms as if she were still a child. All that affection could do was done for her, the turn was taken, and she struggled back to life, though not to health. As soon as she was fit to take charge of the baby he was brought back to her, and was a great source of joy and interest to his young mother. He was a strong child, and soon became an active, noisy little fellow, who often overtaxed Mrs. Glover's strength and proved rather "a handful." Mahala Sanborn and her parents took a great fancy to him, and were always delighted to have his company. Thus it came about that he was much with them, an arrangement which was not productive of good, as they were over-indulgent and let him have too much of his own way.

At this time a great change was taking place in the country. The advent of the railway was breaking down the obstacles which had separated the states of the North-West from those of the North-East; the Alleghanies were crossed, and an easy interchange of commodities replaced the old aloofness of state from state by a new unity founded on business interests. The introduction of machinery gave a great impetus to manufactures, and the attention of New England was gradually turned from agriculture to commerce.

Mr. Baker gave up his farm and took up his abode in Tilton, where he built himself a comfortable house and threw himself with great zest into the affairs of the day. But the family circle was soon to be broken. Mr. Tilton's mills had proved a great success, and his partner George Baker married and went to Baltimore to start a mill there. Less than a year later Mrs. Mark Baker passed away, and in the following year Mr. Baker remarried. In view of this second marriage, it was arranged that Mary should make her home with the Tiltons. She was not strong enough to earn her own living, and her private means were not sufficient to support her and her little boy. Abigail's offer, therefore, seemed the only course open to her, but there was one very distressing condition attached to it. The Tiltons had a child of their own, a boy younger than little George, handsome, but delicate. Mrs. Tilton was delighted to give Mary a home, but she refused to take her boy. Mahala Sanborn was going to be married and would live at North Groton, a place about forty miles away in the mountains; she wished to take George with her, and Mr. Baker and Mrs. Tilton gave their hearty approval to the plan. It seems almost incredibly heartless, for Mrs. Glover was wrapped up in the child, but her entreaties availed nothing, and after a night of agonized prayer she had to part with him. Long years afterwards, Mrs. Eddy spoke of Mahala as "a good girl, kind and tender," but though she was incapable of resentment and could rise above sorrow, she had not yet learned how to rise above ill-health. It is not surprising to learn that from this time her weakness increased and developed into a spinal complaint, accompanied by attacks of complete nervous prostration.

Though weak in body and often confined to bed, Mrs. Glover's mental activity and keenness were in no way impaired. We have seen her as a child carrying on her studies alone, eager for information, an ardent listener as well as full of fun, and ready to play her part in the social doings of the family circle. So during her short married life with George Glover, she was not too engrossed in her new found happiness, the pleasure of her young husband's society, the amusement of starting a house of her own, of meeting his many friends, to be able to ignore the great question of slavery, and fearlessly she raised her voice and employed her pen in exposing and denouncing "the peculiar institution" of the South.

In Miss Wilbur's biography a very interesting incident is recorded of this period. The Tiltons had invited all the notables of the neighbourhood to a reception; the political situation was keenly discussed; Mrs. Glover was present assisting her sister in her duties as hostess, beautiful and graceful in spite of her delicate health, taking no part in the general conversation till directly questioned by one of the guests: "And what does Mrs. Glover have to say to all this?" he asked. "I say," she replied, "that the South as well as the North suffers from the continuance of slavery and its spread to other states; that the election of Franklin Pierce will but involve us in larger disputes; that emancipation is written on the wall."

"Mary," cried her sister, "do you dare to say that in my house?"

"I dare to speak what I believe in any house," was the response, all the more striking from the quiet tone in which it was uttered.

These words were spoken at a time when the political atmosphere of the United States was brewing up for the great storm which for four awful years was to devastate the country. Feeling ran very high; the Fugitive Slave Law had been passed in 1850, by which escaped slaves could be pursued into non-slavery states and brought back without trial by jury; "Uncle Tom's Cabin" had appeared during 1852; several years later Charles Sumner, the Abolitionist, was surprised at his desk in the Senate House and severely beaten by a Southerner. It required no little courage to speak as Mary Glover had spoken.

From the age of eighteen Mary had written for the papers, and at the period under review we hear of her writing political articles for the *New Hampshire Patriot*, and for leading magazines of both the South and the North. In addition to this she was offered a permanent and well-paid post on the staff of *The Odd Fellows' Covenant*, though she did not see her way to accept the position. She also taught for a time in one of the best schools of New Hampshire, with the result that she was recommended to open an infants' school, but her views on the teaching of little children were in advance of the time, and the school did not meet with the success it deserved.

CHAPTER III

IN Mrs. Eddy's Message to The Mother Church for 1901 (p. 26) she writes: "What I have given to the world on the subject of metaphysical healing or Christian Science is the result of my own observation, experience, and final discovery, quite independent of all other authors except the Bible." In "Retrospection and Introspection" (p. 24) she writes: "During twenty years prior to my discovery [of Christian Science] I had been trying to trace all physical effects to a mental cause; and in the latter part of 1866 I gained the scientific certainty that all causation was Mind, and every effect a mental phenomenon." The discovery of Christian Science was made in 1866, so the experiments to which she here alludes must have been begun about the year 1846, when she was living at home, in the first years of her widowhood. After her marriage to Dr. Patterson in 1853, she began the investigation of homœopathy.

We have already heard that homœopathy was first brought to her notice by her cousin, Dr. Morrill, when she was about eighteen years old. She had never been strong, and had found the allopathic medicine which had been prescribed for her disagreeable and ineffectual. With her father's permission she tried homœopathy. As she had been much benefited by her cousin's treatment at this time, it was natural that many years later, when she was suffering from ill-health, she should resort to homœopathy again. She determined to study the subject for herself, and set to work with her usual vigour and perseverance. After a time she began to take patients, and met with much encouragement and considerable success, but the further she went in her studies the more uncertain she became as to what it was that really effected the cures.

As is well known, homœopathy teaches that a disease is cured by the same drug which is capable of causing the disease; that the dose prescribed as the remedy must be smaller than that capable of producing the disease, and that the drug must be administered individually, not compounded with other drugs, as one drug may neutralize or change the action of another. Hahnemann was the first to present this system to the world in general, though from very early times there had been physicians who held that in certain cases "likes should be treated by likes." In 1835 Hahnemann left Germany, where his teachings had met with much opposition, and settled in Paris, where he carried on a successful practice till his death in 1843. He began by using a few grains of the drug at a time, but soon came to see that a much smaller dose was sufficient, though the amount that produced the best effects varied with the patient.

At the time when Mrs. Patterson began the study

of this subject, high attenuations were in great favour, that is, doses in which the drug had been diluted to such an extent that the original properties had completely disappeared. Yet she had found in her practice that serious cases of illness could be cured by these high attenuations, cases some of which had neither been relieved by larger homœopathic doses nor by the prescriptions of allopathy. It was also recognized by homœopathists that the moral and mental symptoms of a case must be taken into account when prescribing for an invalid, and that the higher natures were those most benefited by these infinitesimal doses.

How could this be accounted for? What did the higher attenuations possess which was lacking in the lower attenuations? The making of the higher attenuations occupied much more time and attention. The preparation was shaken thirty times at each attenuation, and every time it was shaken the thought naturally presented itself that by this process the remedy was being made more powerful. Thus it was plainly mind action, and not matter, which effected the cure. Thus far Mrs. Patterson had seen, but she desired to go further to see the nature of the mental action thus brought to bear on the patient. In "Miscellaneous Writings" (p. 379) she says, "I had already experimented in medicine beyond the basis of *materia medica*, — up to the highest attenuation in homœopathy, thence to a mental standpoint not understood, and with phenomenally good results;

meanwhile, assiduously pondering the solution of this great question: Is it matter, or is it Mind, that heals the sick?" Elsewhere she describes three of these experiments.

One of these she tells about in "Christian Healing" (p. 13) as follows: "We have attenuated a grain of aconite until it was no longer aconite, then dropped into a tumblerful of water a single drop of this harmless solution, and administering one teaspoonful of this water at intervals of half an hour have cured the incipient stage of fever."

On another occasion she cured a very serious case of dropsy in the following manner:

The case was considered a hopeless one, and had been given up by the doctor. Mrs. Patterson prescribed the fourth attenuation of Sulphuris. An improvement was soon visible, but as Mrs. Patterson heard that the same remedy had been administered by the doctor who had previously been in charge of the case, she feared that the woman might suffer from a too prolonged use of the medicine, and wished her to give it up. This the patient was afraid to do, so Mrs. Patterson, without telling her of her intention, gave her unmedicated pellets, and the improvement continued as before. After a time the patient agreed to try to do without the pellets, but on the third day felt ill again, and was relieved by resorting once more to the unmedicated pellets. These she continued to take till she was completely restored to health.

The next question that presented itself to her was this: Is it the Mind which was in Christ Jesus which does the healing, or is the agent the human mind and human will? She was unable to answer this momentous question, but she continued to pray earnestly, as had always been her wont, to be kept from sin, and soon made up her mind to investigate the claims of spiritualism, mesmerism and hypnotism.

Modern spiritualism may be said to have had its birth in the State of New York in the year 1848. A family of the name of Fox took a house in Hydesville, and found themselves annoyed by strange noises and movements of the furniture, which they supposed must result from some tricks which were being played upon them, or from some ordinary cause. Failing to find out how these sounds and disturbances arose, they consulted some of their neighbours, but their investigations proved equally unsuccessful. After a time it became apparent that the loudest noises and the most violent movements took place in the presence of, or in close proximity to, the little daughters of Mr. Fox, fourteen and eleven years of age. After this the children were closely watched and subjected to a number of tests to determine whether the noises and movements were caused by any conscious action on their part. These girls, Margaret and Kate Fox, were the first persons ever known as mediums. The investigators began to perceive some method or system in the noises, and assuming that some code of signals was being employed, tried the alphabet, and found that by counting the taps different letters were obtained which formed consecutive sentences. The messages thus rapped out in Mr. Fox's house purported to come from the spirit of a man who had been murdered there.

It was at much the same time that other mediums were discovered in different parts of the country, the spiritualistic phenomena connected with them varying very considerably one from the other. Some mediums when in a state of trance prescribed for patients and had considerable success in healing; some saw figures or heard voices and received messages, while other people in the same room heard and saw nothing out of the common.

Although from the earliest times there have been people who believed in ghosts, and though there are early records of strange happenings of just the same kind as those produced by mediums, the extraordinary development of these phenomena attracted a great deal of attention in Europe as well as in America. Spiritualism was one of the topics of the hour; learned and well-known people investigated the subject, and many persons were convinced that the manifestations had no connection with conjuring tricks or with anything of that nature, and that they afforded veritable and tangible proofs of the immortality of man and of the reality of the spiritual world.

We have seen that great changes had been taking

place in the outward condition of the United States, changes largely brought about through the agency of steam; things which a few years before would have been considered impossible were now being accomplished every day; nothing seemed too wonderful to be true. A great change had also been taking place in the religious thought of the time. Unitarianism and Universalism had established themselves in the New England over which the uncompromising Calvanism of the Puritans had hitherto held sway.

The hold of the old orthodoxy had been loosened, and the subject of spiritualism soon attracted a large following. Mrs. Patterson was a discoverer, looking for a long lost trail through a tangled wilderness, and determined to investigate every path which might lead in the right direction. All her investigations were conducted in the true scientific spirit; she brought to bear on her researches patience, perseverance, alertness, a high degree of capacity, balance and the quality of "intellectual good order," as it was called by a distinguished mental specialist with whom she had an interview when she was eighty-six years of age. To these qualities must be added the unusual ability to distinguish between men and systems, to appreciate the humanity, philanthropy and good qualities of many from whom she differed profoundly in matters religious and philosophic.

From her first investigations of spiritualism, though she did not attribute the spiritualistic phenomena in every case merely to tricks and chicanery, she became convinced that there was nothing scientific about it and nothing spiritual. She was confident that there must be some ordinary, natural explanation of mediumship and of the curious manifestations accompanying it, but it was not till after her discovery of Christian Science that the matter became clear to her. "When I learned how mind produces disease on the body, I learned how it produces the manifestations ignorantly imputed to spirits," she wrote in "Christian Healing" (p. 6).

In Christian Science teaching, Spirit is a synonym for God and should be used in no other sense, hence that which is like God is spiritual, and conversely that which does not express God's nature cannot be spiritual. All Christians are agreed on the point that God is without parts and passions, that He is necessarily invisible to mortal sight; from this it follows that nothing capable of being materially discerned can be spiritual. A scent or odour may suddenly recall a scene long forgotten, or reproduce the sensations and outlook on life of one's nursery days, but we see nothing supernatural in that. Men can despatch messages by the means of wireless telegraphy across the wastes of ocean; the phonograph enables us to hear the voice of the singer or statesman who has passed from this world, but it cannot tell us what music now delights the ear of the singer nor show us the new vista of possibilities opening up to the thought of the statesman. In the same way the communications transmitted by so-called spirits only deal with matters on our present plane of experience, or with the conjectures and speculations concerning a future life entertained by ordinary mortals, even though outwardly unexpressed. Steam is no more spiritual than water or ice, but it is a less dense form of matter, so ghostly apparitions differ in no way from other material phenomena except in their density. Mrs. Eddy writes in Science and Health (p. 86): "Seeing is no less a quality of physical sense than feeling. Then why is it more difficult to see a thought than to feel one? Education alone determines the difference. In reality there is none."

Mrs. Patterson had been brought up in a Puritan household. From her earliest years she had been taught that man can communicate directly with God; she had found this to be true, for she had herself known this spiritual intercourse; how, then, could she accept the belief that man can be enabled to draw nearer to God through the agency of wires, electricity or the spirits of the departed?

Christian Science shows us that there is a way by which the great facts of God's nature can be demonstrated to man, and that this is the way pointed out by Jesus Christ. The healing works performed by our Lord and his disciples were proofs of the truths they taught. The desire felt by spiritualists to bring home to the sceptic some tangible proof of immortality is thus met and satisfied by the healing work of Christian Science.

The human craving to know more of the departed, to learn something of their present surroundings, to know whether it is well with them, is satisfied as the Christian Science student becomes ever more and more conscious from his own experience that divine Love is infinite and universal; believing less in matter and depending less on it, he becomes more aware of the relationship between God and His spiritual creation, and perceives something of the *modus operandi* by which men are sustained and blest.

Thus he realizes that the same tender care which supplied his own helpless infancy with mother, home, food and raiment is still guiding the footsteps of the beloved, in sunshine or in mirk, along the natural paths of a home universe.

"If I ascend up into heaven, thou art there: if I make my bed in hell, behold, thou art there" (Psalms 139:8).

He becomes also convinced that the shortest road to the happy reunion of his heart's desire is the way of God's appointing.

Christian Science teaches that there is but one controlling Mind, and that as each one of us becomes convinced of this fundamental fact, he will be lifted above the chances and changes of this mortal life, and taste of the peace which the world can neither give nor take away. As the sense of "self" becomes less obtrusive, the individual will begin to reflect more of God's nature. Thus it will surely come to pass that when the Science of Christianity is more fully understood and more fully practised, the true Christian, like the prophets and apostles of old, will express an ever-increasing sense of intelligence, wisdom and fore-thought, and will manifest powers and capacities at present unknown.

Mary Glover's marriage to Daniel Patterson held promise of better things. A dentist by profession and a cousin of her stepmother, he had shown a kindly interest in her and her affairs. He assured Mrs. Tilton and Mark Baker that he would be able to restore Mary to health if she would but marry him. Her separation from her boy, he declared, was the chief factor in her illness; the restoration of her child, combined with his personal care and homœopathic treatment, would make her well. The family was in favour of the marriage, and Mary was induced to consent, chiefly from the desire to regain her son.

The Pattersons' married life began with a broken promise. Dr. Patterson refused to allow little George to live with them, on the old pretence that Mary was not strong enough yet to stand his high spirits. For two years they lived at Franklin, Mrs. Patterson being left much alone, while her husband travelled about on his professional rounds from village to village. Then Dr. Patterson moved to North Groton, partly to please his wife, who longed to be near the

Cheneys, with whom George lived, and here mother and son met once more. Her happiness at having the boy with her can be more easily imagined than described. He was now twelve years old. He took a great fancy to her, and was frequently in the house, to the displeasure of the Cheneys and Dr. Patterson, who appeared to be jealous of their affection one for the other. Finally, Mrs. Tilton was informed that George's society was injuriously affecting his mother's health; she arrived in North Groton, and shortly afterwards the Cheneys moved to Minnesota, taking the boy with them. This was bad enough, but worse was to follow. A deliberate plot was formed to separate them finally. George was informed that his mother was dead; she was told that he was lost, and though she took every step in her power, she could find out nothing about him. A woman without money, suffering from a severe spinal ailment, with her family in league against her, how, indeed, could she trace a boy fifteen hundred miles away? Her strong faith in God's goodness prevented her from succumbing to despair, but it is not surprising to hear that her health grew still worse.

Of the four years that followed there is little to tell. Dr. Patterson was often away from home, and when with her was no real companion. He was considered an unusually skilful dentist, but he was not a man of refinement or principle, and was constantly in money difficulties.

We have seen his behaviour in the matter of his little step-son, but in other ways he was kind to her, as her own words testify. During her husband's absences, Mrs. Patterson had often no other companionship but that of her little blind maid, who was tenderly attached to her and very attentive; but even though circumscribed by ill-health and lack of fortune, Mary's spirit remained unbroken. She continued her search for health, submitting herself to the most rigorous system of hygiene and diet and trying homœopathic treatment. She read, she wrote, she coached a neighbour's fifteen year old boy in elementary mathematics and physics, and constantly meditated on the subject of causation and the so-called miracles of the Bible. On one occasion her own health took a sudden turn for the better, but the improvement was not sustained; on another occasion she was able instantaneously to restore to sight a blind baby, and she strove to understand how these cures had been brought about, but so far in vain; the answer to her questions still remained veiled and obscure.

In the autumn of 1861, Dr. Patterson became interested in the reports which reached him of a certain Phineas P. Quimby, of Portland, Maine, who was said to be performing very remarkable cures. Some called him a mere quack or impostor, others maintained that he was a scientific man who had made some valuable discoveries on the treatment of disease. Dr. Patterson wrote to him about his wife's complaint and received an answer declaring that he had no doubt of being able to heal her if she came to him for treatment. Dr. Patterson was quite inclined to take Mary to Portland to visit Dr. Quimby, but delayed doing this; and in the spring of 1862, after the outbreak of the war, he was taken prisoner by Southern soldiers while viewing a battlefield in Virginia. Mrs. Patterson heard of her husband's fate from the newspapers, and at once exerted herself to procure his release, but without success.

The Republican party had been formed a few years before the date with which we are now dealing by a fusion of Democrats and Whigs and a large number of quite young men who had had no previous party affiliation. The bond which held them together was their resolution to resist any further encroachments on the part of the supporters of slavery. Their first leader was John Charles Fremont, "The Pathfinder," who had done so much to open up the Far West of America. He was defeated by James Buchanan, whose four years' administration included some of the darkest days of the country's history. But the Republican party was growing in strength, and when in 1860 the Southern vote was split by the appearance of three Democratic candidates for the Presidency, the election of a Republican was assured. The party choice fell upon Abraham Lincoln. The presidential election held in November brought the question of slavery to a climax, and the South determined on secession. In December South Carolina called a convention which repealed the ordinance in which the Constitution of the United States had been adopted by her in 1788. On the 8th of February the States of Florida, Georgia, Alabama, Mississippi, Louisiana, Texas and South Carolina declared themselves the Confederate States of America, with Jefferson Davis as President, but even this act did not lead to immediate war. On the 4th of March, Lincoln was inaugurated — that is he entered upon his duties as President — and a month was spent in earnest deliberation as to the course which should be adopted. The special matter under consideration concerned the forts in Charleston Harbor, South Carolina, to which the Confederate States laid claim, and the first shot of the Civil War was fired when the Confederacy ordered an attack on Fort Sumter. After gallantly holding out for a day and a half, Major Anderson and his little garrison were obliged to surrender, and the Civil War began.

There were many people in the North who would have been glad to get rid of the problem of slavery by allowing the Confederate States to go on their way, and still more who, while deploring the break up of the Union, felt that even that might be preferable to Civil War, but the attack on Fort Sumter so welded the North together that Lincoln's call for men to defend the Union met with an enthusiastic response.

George Glover, though only sixteen years old, answered his country's call, and enlisted at the outbreak of war, and was sent to the front. Later he learned that his mother was alive. He wrote to her, and we can well image her happiness at hearing from him and the tears of joy which she shed over the pages of his precious letter! Her hopes, however, were once more doomed to be dashed; he again passed out of her ken, and Mrs. Eddy tells us in "Retrospection and Introspection" (p. 21) that she never met him again till he was thirty-four years old, with a wife and two children. He was wounded at the battle of Shiloh, served during the four years of the Civil War, and as a reward for his services was afterwards given a Government appointment in the Territory of Dakota.

CHAPTER IV

THE next event of importance in Mrs. Patterson's life was the visit which she paid to Dr. Quimby in October, 1862. During the dark and anxious months which followed on the outbreak of the Civil War, with her son in the thick of the fighting, and her husband a prisoner, whilst she herself was largely confined to bed, Mrs. Patterson turned more and more to the study of the Bible, and of the cases of healing recorded in its pages. The conviction was becoming stronger and stronger that there must be a spiritual law behind these works of healing, a law which could be rediscovered and utilized for the benefit of the sick. The thought, too, kept presenting itself that perhaps Dr. Quimby had rediscovered this law, that his cures might be effected by this means, and as this feeling grew, so did the desire to see him and talk with him grow, till at last she resolved, in spite of the great difficulties in the way, to take the journey to Portland and see for herself. It was impossible to take this step without informing her sister, Mrs. Tilton, of her intentions and getting her assistance, so Mary laid the matter before her. As might have been expected, Mrs. Tilton was much opposed to the project. She declared that Quimby was a quack, a mesmerist, a man of no education. If Mary wished to try a new course of treatment, she insisted that it should be something respectable, well thought of, and regular. Let her go to Dr. Vail's Hydropathic Institute in their own State. In vain Mary pointed out that she had tried medical and hygienic treatment for a period of years without effect. Abigail insisted, and at last the younger sister gave way. She had been over two months at the Hydropathic Institute, following the course prescribed, but getting steadily worse, when she met a man, previously considered incurable, who had just returned from Portland, restored to health by Dr. Quimby's treatment. His case naturally excited much interest, and Mrs. Patterson and several other of Dr. Vail's patients left the Institute and journeyed to Portland to put themselves under Quimby's care.

Mrs. Patterson's first meeting with Dr. Quimby took place in October, 1862, at the International Hotel, Portland, where he had a suite of rooms in which he received his patients. Miss Wilbur describes how Mrs. Patterson's earnest gaze fell upon the man whom she had so ardently desired to see. She writes of him as "healthy, dominant, energetic," with "shrewd, penetrating eyes," a kindly face and sincere expression. The treatment which he proceeded to give was preluded by a few explanations. "He told her . . . that she was held in bondage by the opinion of her family and physicians, that her animal spirit

[43]

was reflecting its grief upon her body and calling it spinal disease." As he said these words he looked her full in the eyes, and then proceeded to dip his hands in water and rub her head violently in order to impart healthy electricity. Almost at once the burden of pain and weakness which she had so long borne about with her fell away, and a sense of well-being rushed in and took its place.

It seemed to her that at last her prayers were answered, and that this restoration to health was a proof that the healing was of God. Her gratitude to Quimby was unbounded, for she was convinced that he had rediscovered the spiritual healing of the Gospel, and she proceeded with her wonted enthusiasm to attempt the impossible task of connecting his treatment with the teachings of our Lord and his disciples. Later she found that her health was not firmly established, her recovery was not permanent, and various ailments kept returning. It seems as if the joy of Mrs. Patterson's recovery was so great that for the time the critical faculty was in abeyance, and it took her several years before she saw clearly that Quimby's methods were only a variety of mesmerism.

Dr. Quimby himself denied that he then made use of mesmerism, but in "The Quimby Manuscripts" later published by Mr. H. W. Dresser, he is quoted as saying: "I found that by the power of my own mind I could change the mind of my patient." He also says that he finds out the patient's fears and feelings through clairvoyance, then throws these feelings off, and imparts to the patient his own healthy feelings. His treatment, therefore, was largely what we would now call "suggestion," for all mental treatment which is not founded on the understanding that there is but one Mind, God, can only be a form of mesmerism, however little the operator may be aware of this.

Mrs. Patterson remained three weeks in Portland, having daily talks with Dr. Quimby, and then returned to her sister's home in Tilton, believing herself restored to health and over-flowing with gratitude. She told everyone of her experience, and spoke so enthusiastically that Mrs. Tilton was prompted to ask Quimby to treat her son, who had taken to unsatisfactory habits. She took young Tilton to Portland at least twice to put him under treatment, but, apparently, he was not benefited, and his mother and Mrs. Samuel Baker, who had accompanied Mrs. Patterson on her visit to Portland to look into Dr. Quimby's system of healing, pronounced it the essence of quackery.

Not long after this Dr. Patterson escaped from prison and returned to her. He had endured much in his captivity and felt disinclined to settle down immediately and resume his dental practice, so while he was paying visits and lecturing on his prison experiences, Mary made her headquarters with Mrs. Tilton, and engaged with her in work for the soldiers.

She also visited friends and her husband's relatives in Maine.

She went to see Dr. Quimby in 1863, several times in 1864, and again in 1865, as she was anxious to gain a clearer sense of his philosophy and method of healing, but this desire necessarily remained unsatisfied since he did not understand it himself. In the summer of the year 1864, Dr. Patterson having at last taken an office and settled in Lynn, his wife was able to rejoin him.

In outward matters, Mrs. Patterson's position seemed greatly improved. Residence in Lynn made a pleasant change after the small country villages in which she had been living for so long. The town is only eleven miles from Boston, a busy, thriving place, pleasantly situated on the sea. Here she made some lasting friendships with people of refinement and culture, wrote a good deal for the local press, took a leading part in temperance work, and was made President of the Legion of Honor, the woman's branch of the Good Templars. Yet, in spite of these pleasant circumstances, writing of this time, Mary spoke of it as the darkest period of her life. There was no silver lining to the clouds which hung over her, she said. There was no hope anywhere. "The world was dark. The oncoming hours were indicated by no floral dial. The senses could not prophesy sunrise or starlight" (Retrospection and Introspection, p. 23). How is this to be accounted for?

The temporary relief which followed Mrs. Patterson's first visit to Dr. Quimby led her to think that in this matter he was an instrument of heaven. After her discovery of Christian Science she began to see the great chasm which separates the healing of God from mental cures which are not based on the divine nature and power. Then she was enabled to separate the great personal kindness of the man from the dangerous system which he ignorantly practised, the mists which his treatment had engendered were dispelled, and she was able to warn others of the effects of mesmerism. Even where, as in Quimby's case, the motives of the mesmerist are wholly benevolent, Christian Science maintains that all such treatment is injurious. It can only cure a man of illness by substituting therefor a greater error — the effect of personal control, so that the last state of the patient is worse than the first.

As for Dr. Quimby, he fell a victim to his own system. In October, 1865, a Mr. Clark came to him asking for assistance, and was treated by him daily for a month. At the end of that time he told Mrs. Clark that he could not cure her husband, nor get rid for himself of the illness which he had drawn out of Mr. Clark. None of his friends were able to assist him, and he succumbed to the disease in the January following (1866).

The year 1865 had been a very eventful one in the national history. In March, Lincoln had been inaugurated as President for a second term of four years; in April, Lee, the great leader of the Southern or Confederate forces, was obliged to surrender to General Ulysses Grant, and the Civil War was at an end. America had lost of her children in this terrible struggle over 280,000 men, but the Union was intact, and the curse of slavery swept from the land. For one brief week the North rejoiced; sorrow for the gallant lads who had passed from this world was tempered by the great happiness of knowing that their supreme sacrifice had not been made in vain; Lincoln was already engaged on plans for the restoration of the country, full of kindness and good-will even to those who had caused and inaugurated the war, anxious as soon as it could be done with safety to "let bygones be bygones," when a fresh blow fell. He was assassinated when seated with his wife and a few friends in a box at the theatre.

Less than six weeks after Lincoln's murder, the armies of the North were ordered to Washington. For two days the youthful veterans passed through the capital amidst sobered crowds whose gratitude for peace was none the less profound; and then the disbanding began. Most of the men were quickly paid off and returned to their homes and to peaceful occupations. It was a wonderful proof of the spirit which called into existence and animated the Federal forces, that the disbanding was accomplished with such rapidity and ease.

In the little volume of Poems by Mary Baker
Eddy, published in 1910, appear some lines written
"To the Old Year—1865." They are very solemn
in tone. In one verse occur the following words:

"Say, will the young year dawn with wisdom's light
To brighten o'er thy bier?"

This question was soon to be answered.

On the evening of the 1st of February, 1866,
Mrs. Patterson was on her way to attend a temperance
meeting in Lynn. The night was frosty and the roads
covered with ice; she slipped and fell with such vio-
lence as to be rendered insensible. In this state she was
carried into a near-by house and a doctor summoned.
He said that she was suffering from a concussion of
the brain, and that she had also injured her spine.
Mrs. Patterson remained unconscious all night, but
recovered sufficient consciousness in the morning to
be able to moan "home." She was in great suffering,
but was wrapped in furs and conveyed on a sleigh as
carefully as possible to the house in Swampscott
where she and her husband were then residing.

On the following Sunday morning, before pro-
ceeding to his service, the minister whose church she
attended came to bid her farewell, for she was considered to be at the point of death. Mrs. Patterson
asked the friends who had assembled in her sick
room to leave her alone with the Bible; the pages
opened at the passage in St. Matthew's Gospel (9:2),

in which is given the account of our Lord's healing of the man with the palsy. She read, and lo! the bridegroom came! Something for which she had been waiting and longing all her life roused her, took possession of her. A new sense of being must have filled her consciousness.

"The divine hand led me into a new world of light and Life, a fresh universe — old to God, but new to His 'little one,' " she writes in "Retrospection and Introspection" (p. 27). She became aware, she tells us in "Science and Health with Key to the Scriptures" (p. 108), that "all real being is in God, the divine Mind, and that Life, Truth, and Love are all-powerful and ever-present." Our Lord's character, the inner meaning of his words and works were suddenly illuminated, and she was restored to better health. She had had revealed to her something hitherto concealed by the mists of false belief; she had come into touch with the law of Spirit, and behold the body was reconstructed, but how this miracle had been wrought, what the *modus operandi* of this law, she could not say. Nine years of experience and proof, nine years of ceaseless toil and earnest prayer were to pass before she was prepared to give Science and Health to the world, and before the world was ready to receive it.

God's ways are not man's ways. If Christian Science be, indeed, what its students claim it to be, this healing of a middle-aged woman, in a modest home just outside a manufacturing town of New England, has marked a new era in history, has started the greatest mental revolution since the Apostolic Age, has brought to bear on the fortunes of men and nations forces which have lain hidden and unsuspected for long centuries.

It is not yet seventy years since the discovery of Christian Science,* and during that time it has gained adherents in every quarter of the globe and its progressive influence has had a leavening effect on the medical and religious views of large numbers of those outside the movement.

Every new discovery encounters incredulity and opposition, and Mrs. Patterson's discovery was no exception to this rule. She dressed herself and walked into the neighbouring room where her friends were assembled awaiting her death. They were profoundly startled; they almost took her for a ghost, but, delighted as they were to have her restored to health, they could not accept her declaration that she had been raised from her death bed by the direct power of God. To them the acts of healing recorded in the Bible were miracles; they were convinced that the age of miracles had passed, and they had no wish to have their views on such subjects disturbed.

The Pattersons were standing at the parting of the ways. This great spiritual light which had fallen on Mary's path, revealing, though at first dimly, the

*Mrs. Eddy discovered Christian Science in 1866.

upward track for which she had been searching all her life long, this light which was filling her with joy and calling her to a higher and more spiritual life, produced a totally different effect on one whose interests were wholly centred on the things of this world. Dr. Patterson took the downward path. He eloped shortly afterwards with the wife of a well-known resident of Lynn. The woman subsequently returned to her husband, and Dr. Patterson would have liked to resume life with his wife, but she could not consent, and later obtained a divorce.

After Dr. Patterson's departure, Mrs. Tilton wrote to ask her sister to come and live next door to her, offering to build her a suitable house; but she attached a condition to this otherwise attractive proposal to which Mary could not agree. She must promise to attend the Tiltons' church and to give up her theory of divine healing. By this condition, she found herself cut off from home and relations, alone in the world. Her father had passed away over a year before; her son was lost to her. The old life was utterly gone; an unknown future was opening before her. We get some glimpses from the verses she wrote at this time of her hard struggle with heart-ache and the human longing for affection and home, but she had little time to spend in self-pity or vain regrets; she had heard the call of God, and must go forward "forgetting those things which are behind" (Philippians 3:13).

As has been stated already, though she had been instantaneously restored to better health by a sense of God's presence hitherto unknown, she had still to understand the Science of her healing and to learn how this Science could be explained to others and rendered available for all mankind. In order to follow up and elucidate her discovery, she must have leisure and quiet, but her limited means of about two hundred dollars a year did not leave her much choice of residence. Her first place of abode was with a family of the name of Clark, who took in boarders. Here Mrs. Glover, as she now preferred to be called, received a kindly welcome, and was left free to spend as much time as she chose in the seclusion of her own room. The first people to whom she presented her experience in Christian Science were, naturally, her personal friends. These held an honoured place in the community as leading citizens of high character and culture. She performed remarkable cures among them, but they were not able to grasp her teachings nor willing to put this new Science to the test.

In order to gain some conception as to how these cures were effected, it is necessary to understand what Christian Science teaches on the following points.

All Christians hold that God is Spirit, the only creator, ever-present, all-powerful, infinite and omniscient. Christian Science points out that if God is omniscient and infinite, He must also be infinite intelligence or all the intelligence there is; He must, therefore, be the one and only Mind. Thus it maintains that men do not possess private separate minds of their own, that each one has the capacity to reflect the intelligence which is God, if he only knows that it is so.

In Mrs. Eddy's own words in Science and Health (p. 330), "God is infinite, the only Life, substance, Spirit, or Soul, the only intelligence of the universe, including man. Eye hath neither seen God nor His image and likeness. Neither God nor the perfect man can be discerned by the material senses. The individuality of Spirit, or the infinite, is unknown, and thus a knowledge of it is left either to human conjecture or to the revelation of divine Science." Jesus, she defines as "The highest human corporeal concept of the divine idea, rebuking and destroying error and bringing to light man's immortality" (Science and Health, p. 589).

What, then, is matter? God is Spirit, Mind, therefore His creation must be mental, or it could not be like its creator. Like produces like, nothing can be expressed in effect which is not contained in cause. Matter is in every respect the opposite of Spirit. A mortal body is imperfect, impermanent, and cannot be the outcome of perfection and immortality. The matter we see around us in our waking hours is no more real than the matter we see in our dreams. In the night dream we meet men and women; these dream people appear to have life in their bodies, intelligence, activity, and yet when that change of consciousness takes place which we call "awakening," we perceive that the objects, the people, the circumstances of our dream were but illusions, fancies. Our sense of life, intelligence, activity, was false; these forces were not in the dream people. Life, intelligence, activity, Christian Science contends, are no more in matter than are truth and honour. They are emanations from the nature of God, reflected by man and beast.

Christian Science teaches the unreliable nature of the testimony of the material senses; it teaches that we should look beneath the surface of things, and so find the causes which produce the outward and visible; it declares that it can enable us to distinguish between true causation and those false beliefs, that incorrect reasoning, confused thinking, and fear from which all the trouble in the world proceeds. Mrs. Glover's own experiences had shown her that whenever she had become sufficiently conscious of the nature of God, the omnipotent, ever-present, and all-wise, this sense of God's presence had cast out some particular fear and the outward form in which it had manifested itself. Thus in her childhood's experience of spiritual healing, the mental perturbation inspired by the relentless doctrine of fore-ordination and eternal damnation expressed itself outwardly as a fever, and it was "the angel of his presence" (Isaiah

63:9), the sudden consciousness of God's infinite compassion and tenderness, which cast out the distress and its outward expression the fever.

It will thus be seen that the system called Christian Science is wholly based on the spiritual nature of God and man as revealed in the Bible; that it claims to be the Science of Mind, and maintains that every form of evil, of sin, sorrow and illness is in the absolute sense of the term, unreal, because not procured by God. Further, it declares that illness and disaster of all sorts are the outward expression of mistaken thinking, of false thoughts held consciously or unconsciously, and that the only satisfactory way of permanently getting rid of these outward evils is by the detection and correction of the erroneous thought which produced them. In this way, Christian Science teaches, the body is "transformed by the renewing of [the] mind" (Rom. 12:2).

Moreover, it teaches that since God is the only cause and creator, and the only Mind of the universe, He must necessarily be the only law-giver and the only law. Thus God governs the universe and man by spiritual law, the law of His own nature. Once this great fact is grasped, physical laws begin to lose their seeming power, and the miracles of the Bible are seen, not as contraventions of the law, but as demonstrations of an ever-operative law of Spirit, long hidden and now once more made known to mankind.

Toward the end of 1866, Mrs. Glover had gained the conviction that "all causation was Mind, and every effect a mental phenomenon" (Retrospection and Introspection, p. 24). By 1867 she had also found someone as eager to learn, as she was to teach, these first revealings of Christian Science. Hiram Crafts and his wife were among the boarders at the Clarks' house. He was a shoemaker, a first-class heel-finisher, who had come to Lynn to work in one of the factories there. His place at table was next to Mrs. Glover, and he listened to her talk with ever-growing interest and enthusiasm. The possibility of a closer walk with God, for which he had been hungering all his life, made an irresistible appeal to him. He was convinced that Christian Science was the truth, and opened his heart to accept it with a child's simple faith. When first Mrs. Glover began the study of Christian Science, she tells us that she knew not how to express in clear, comprehensible language, the thronging, half-formed thoughts which were coming to her. This new, wonderful discovery seemed at first like beautiful strains of far-off music, caught but in part. It seemed as if it would take "centuries of spiritual growth" (Miscellaneous Writings, p. 380) to enable her to elucidate or demonstrate her discovery, and yet here was Hiram Crafts, not asking merely for physical healing, but to be taught how to heal others!

Thus Mrs. Glover was forced to begin writing

down for his benefit some simple statements gained from her own experiences, and with the help of these, and through study of the Bible, she began to teach him the elements of Christian Science. Like the prophets of old, she was constantly relying on divine guidance, and so was led to take one successful step after another, even when this action was contrary to her personal judgment. This may seem strange to one unacquainted with Christian Science. Yet if Christianity is a "way" — to give it the name by which it was first called — human sense is as inadequate to guide us along this unknown mental path as it would be incapable of bringing the great ship without compass, sun or star across the wide Atlantic up to her moorings at the Broomielaw. Mrs. Eddy maintained that some surer guide than personal sense is needed, that we must let Christian Science teach us how to understand enough of the Principle of the universe to be able to be guided by it through the changes and chances of this present existence.

Hiram Crafts' eager desire to be taught Christian Science led Mrs. Glover to begin teaching. Her lessons proved so helpful and engrossing, that Crafts abandoned his plan of spending the winter working in the shoe factories of Lynn, and determined to devote himself entirely to the practice of Christian Science. Before engaging in the healing work, he required further instruction and preparation, so he begged Mrs. Glover to come and live with him and his wife in their house at East Stoughton and undertake his further education in Christian Science.

To leave Lynn with the Crafts involved separation from many kind friends, and the surrender for the time being of all intellectual companionship. On the other hand, it was plain that Lynn was not at present ready to accept any teaching so radical and original as Christian Science. There were a great many Quakers, Methodists and Congregationalists in the place, deeply attached to their churches, and convinced of the orthodoxy of their own views, and Mrs. Glover had already become aware of a growing sense of opposition to her and her new doctrines.

Accordingly, after considering Hiram Crafts' proposal carefully, Mrs. Glover came to the conclusion that she should accept it, and so she left Lynn and lived with the Crafts for about nine months, first at East Stoughton and then at Taunton. In the following spring, Crafts opened an office in the latter place, and for some months supported himself and his wife by the practice of Christian Science healing. Thus a further advance towards the establishment of Christian Science had been made; Mrs. Glover had proved that not only could she herself heal the sick by this method, but that she could also impart this understanding to others.

During the four years from 1866 to 1870 Mrs. Glover moved from one place to another, living for a while with one family and then with another. We have descriptions of her and of her manner of life at this time from various people who knew her well, but did not accept her teachings.

In Miss Wilbur's biography appear two interesting passages of this kind, and some other interesting personal reminiscences are given in an article on Lynn, which appeared in *The Christian Science Monitor* of May 11, 1914. These accounts represent Mrs. Glover as a very beautiful woman, with abundance of lovely hair, which she arranged in a becoming manner. She was always dressed tastefully, though with great simplicity. She spent long hours writing and studying in her private room, but when she emerged from its seclusion, she joined in a natural way in whatever was going on. Serene and happy in herself, she took a kindly interest in other people, was large-hearted, generous, tolerant. She loved children, and was loved by them for her brightness, gaiety and kindness. In her leisure hours she allowed the boys to romp about her room, took the girls for delightful country walks, read to them, listened to what they had to say. She gave as little trouble as anyone could give, and whilst markedly of superior education and breeding, gave herself no "airs," and yet she had to leave one house after another because she felt that her presence was no longer welcome. How can this be accounted for?

As has been already stated, Christian Science teaches that God, the first cause or Principle of the universe, is Mind, and that this Mind expresses itself in ideas which naturally partake of the nature of Mind and are made in God's image. Thus all that really exists is mental or spiritual. Man, God's idea, is inseparable from God, has no mind apart from God, but that "which was also in Christ Jesus" (Phil. 2:5). All true thought proceeds from Mind or God, and is received by each individual man through the spiritual senses. Now in the second chapter of Genesis we are presented with an account of the creation which is at all points the antithesis of that set forth in the first chapter. Christian Science explains this second account as an allegory. It begins with a mist, a dream; everything is represented as evolved from lower forms of matter; a sense of evil appears, a delusion, disobedience, fear follows, a sense of separation from God, toil, pain, difficulty, envy, hatred, murder and, finally, the deluge. Thus evil begins with a mist or sense of obscurity, and, St. Paul tells us, will finally be destroyed by "the brightness of his coming." In the original allegory, of course, matter is represented as made by God, for this is the foundation on which the delusion is raised. Were it seen clearly that matter has no God, that is, no cause behind it, it would be seen as a false impression, and would cease to deceive. This Adam dream lasted down the ages till our Lord came and proved the reality of Spirit and the unreality of matter by his wonderful life and deeds. A few of his followers were able to grasp his teachings to a certain degree, and proved their understanding by the healing work which they performed.

St. Paul speaks of the carnal mind as enmity against God. What did he mean by the carnal mind? All thought supposed to emanate from the mortal will and brain. There is but one Mind, therefore all thought which does not proceed from this Mind can be but a false sense of thought, and a false sense of a thing is always at enmity with the truth about a thing.

After long ages Mrs. Glover rediscovered the great fact that all reality is spiritual, and that it is not matter, but simply a belief in matter, which hides out the spiritual facts of being from the eyes of mankind. No one else in the world saw what she saw; hardly anyone cared even to hear her experiences; those who listened, even those who were benefited by her treatment, did not pursue the path. People who had been her friends cooled in their friendship, became unfriendly, even antagonistic without any apparent cause. At first Mrs. Glover could not account for this opposition, but gradually the reason became plain. She saw that all good is one, since all good is of God and God is indivisible; she likewise saw that all evil is one, being but different manifestations of the carnal or mortal mind, of that dream sense which declares that there is something besides infinite, ever-present, omnipotent Spirit.

As her friends and neighbours began to perceive

that the acceptance of Mrs. Glover's teachings would lead to a complete revolution of thought, they began to draw away from her; some turned back, alarmed at the prospect of this new Reformation, some, stirred by jealousy and resentment, turned against her and attempted to stop the progress of the work; whilst others were lulled into apathetic sleep by the unseen action of the carnal mind.

The opposition and persecutions which had pursued the early Reformers could no longer assume the same outward shape in a land where religious freedom was one of the foundation stones of the constitution, but "the despotic tendencies, inherent in mortal mind," are "always germinating in new forms of tyranny," as Science and Health says (p. 225), and opposition to new ideas only assumes more subtle forms.

From 1866 to 1870, Mrs. Glover lived with various families in different towns in Massachusetts. Part of the time she found her home with spiritualists rather than with orthodox church people, because they were more inclined to listen to her, and her one object was to spread abroad this Science which was to heal the sorrows of the world. During these years she performed some wonderful cures.

At Westerly, Rhode Island, where Mrs. Glover had been invited to lecture on Christian Science, she was asked to help a woman whose case had been given up as hopeless by the doctors. The woman was considered to be at the point of death, and preparations for the burial had been made. She was instantaneously restored to health, her baby being born safely, and weighing twelve pounds (see Retrospection and Introspection, p. 40).

Mrs. Glover also performed a remarkable cure in the case of her niece, her sister Martha's daughter, on the occasion of a visit to Tilton. Miss Pilsbury was lying dangerously ill of enteritis when Mrs. Glover entered her room; in about a quarter of an hour's time she was able to rise from bed and walk seven times across her room. The next day she dressed and went downstairs, and on the fourth day took a train journey of about one hundred miles. This case, duly attested by a near relation of the patient, is given along with several others in the earlier editions of Science and Health. But in both these cases the very completeness of the cures stirred up opposition and resentment. In the first instance, it is sad to relate that the clergy and doctors of the place banded together, tore down the notices announcing a second lecture by Mrs. Glover, and refused her the use of any hall in the town. In Miss Pilsbury's case, the opposition did not show itself at once, but she gradually became estranged from her aunt, and ended by taking up a position of the greatest hostility to her and her teachings, even going so far as to persuade her Aunt Abigail in her last illness not to send for her sister Mary.

Many times in Mrs. Glover's experience were our Lord's words fulfilled. "Think not that I am come to send peace on earth: I came not to send peace, but a sword. For I am come to set a man at variance against his father, and the daughter against her mother. . . . And a man's foes shall be they of his own household" (Matthew 10:35, 36).

This wonderful light of Christian Science, as it appeared to her, revealing to the world the spiritual treasures of the Bible long hidden by the dust of superficial religion, bringing the sunlight of hope and heaven to the dark dreary paths of everyday life, seemed to them, viewing it from afar, through a mist of prejudice, but a will o' the wisp, an incomprehensible phantom of the imagination, uncanny, if not positively dangerous.

About the year 1868, Mrs. Glover tells us in her book "Pulpit and Press" (p. 54), she healed the poet Whittier of incipient pulmonary consumption in a single visit. Amongst other cures recorded of this period is one of pneumonia, healed instantaneously, in which the doctor, who had pronounced the case hopeless, expressed his astonishment, and urged Mrs. Glover to write a book on her curative system of metaphysics (see Miscellany, p. 105). As we know, this it was her intention to do, and, indeed, she was at that time occupied in writing a pamphlet called "The Science of Man," which she copyrighted in 1870. This pamphlet was afterwards incorporated in her textbook, "Science and Health with Key to the Scriptures," where it now forms the chapter "Recapitulation." Although "The Science of Man" was copyrighted at this time, it was not published till later, as Mrs. Glover felt that further proof of the efficacy of Christian Science must be presented to the public before there could be a demand for such a work. For eight years, therefore, she was contented to copy out and distribute her manuscript for the use of her students.

Previous to this time, as she tells us in the preface to Science and Health, she had written many notes on passages of Scripture. For three years she had been making a profound study of the Bible; she had read little else, and had devoted all her time and energies to her search for the truth. She had healed many people, and had taught all who were willing to be taught, but she now began to see that a further step must be taken; she must emerge from her seclusion and be prepared to lay her discovery before a larger public. Four years before this she had left Lynn, now she saw that it was time to return thither.

Accordingly, in June, 1870, Mrs. Glover once more went to live in Lynn. She was accompanied by a young man, Richard Kennedy by name, who had become greatly interested in metaphysics, and who wished to pursue his studies in Christian Science under her direction. He proposed to treat patients, while she devoted her time to teaching and writing.

They found suitable rooms and offices in the house of a lady who kept a private school for little girls. Very soon patients began to arrive, and received so much benefit from the treatment that many wished to learn more of the subject. Thus it came about that classes were formed. Up to this time Mrs. Glover's comparatively small charges had not been uniform, and it soon became evident that the small income which had hitherto proved sufficient to meet her modest needs must be augmented in some way if the knowledge of Christian Science was to be further spread abroad. In "The First Church of Christ, Scientist, and Miscellany" (pp. 214, 215) she tells us that she felt sorely oppressed by the seeming difficulties which confronted her. She had no money with which to hire a hall in which to speak; she longed to be able to provide free board and lodging for people who could not otherwise afford to take instruction from her; indeed, the lack of means confronted her in many directions.

In these difficulties she turned, as was her wont, to God, the divine Mind, and it came to her forcibly that she ought to charge a regular sum for class teaching. In the same manner she saw that it was right for her students to charge for their services so that they might be able to devote all their time to the work of Christian Science, and yet be able to support themselves and to contribute to the needs of the work. Later, the proceeds from Science and

Health and her other writings helped to furnish means for future activities.

Christian Science teaches that God is the only cause. He is therefore the source of all supply; man is His image and reflection; he therefore reflects the abundance of God. Whence then comes poverty? It originates in the belief that matter, not Spirit, is the source of supply. On the other hand, a man who recognizes God as the source of supply is daily striving to manifest more of God's nature, to express more honesty, generosity, gratitude, wisdom and love, and these improved thoughts externalize themselves in what we call improved material conditions. The sense of lack disappears as one gains a clearer perception of his own nature, a deeper sense of his unity with God, and a wider sense of freedom and of dominion. Thus the disease called poverty can be healed by the "renewing of [the] mind." Moreover, the constant recognition of God as the source of supply which brings to the poor man better housing, better clothes, greater comfort, brings to the rich man freedom from the trammels of wealth. His tastes become simpler, his needs fewer, and he, too, becomes more conscious of the peace "which passeth all understanding."

As long as we believe in matter as the source of supply we shall also believe that one man's gain is another man's loss, but when we perceive that Spirit is the source of supply, we see that man can have no need which Love cannot supply. In Science and Health (p. 206) it is written, "In the scientific relation of God to man, we find that whatever blesses one blesses all, as Jesus showed with the loaves and the fishes, — Spirit, not matter, being the source of supply." This recognition of the infinity of abundance does more than help its possessor, it helps unconsciously to lift some of his neighbour's burden of fear, and so helps to eliminate his sense of poverty.

CHAPTER V

MRS. GLOVER'S first regular classes were held in July and August, 1870. They took place in the evenings, as most of the students were employed during the day, the larger number in the shoe factories of Lynn. Many of the students took up the healing work as soon as they had passed through the course of instruction and met with such wonderful success that they were almost as surprised at their results as were their patients. But it is, indeed, a true saying that history repeats itself. As it was in the beginning of the Christian era, so was it now, many are called, but few chosen; among Mrs. Eddy's early students few were able to withstand the seen and the unseen opposition of the world to this new Reformation; some found her standard of life too high for them, and returned to their old ways of thinking, whilst others, having seen something of the power of thought, attempted to make use of it for their own ends, and so began to employ manipulation and methods of hypnotism.

Perceiving the dangers which might arise from the manipulation of patients, beginning with the spring of 1872, Mrs. Glover absolutely forbade the practice. Several students refused to obey, and left her. It became evident that they were relying on manipulation, and not on Christian Science. Later, Richard Kennedy, one of her earliest pupils, stated that his cures were accomplished by energetic rubbing of the head, and that this method had been taught him by Mrs. Glover. It is a well-known fact that Mrs. Glover had never manipulated a patient, whilst subsequent events showed that the manipulation was employed by him in order to gain control over the patient, who thereafter became dependent on him, and the tool of his will.

Before matters came to an open rupture, she had tried in vain, over and over again, to show this pupil something of what was being unfolded to her mental vision; but as nothing can be placed in a closed fist, so a closed consciousness can receive nothing. This parting with Richard Kennedy was but the first of many such partings, for few were prepared to make the sacrifice of self which Christian Science demanded. They began with enthusiasm, full of joy and confidence in the future, full of gratitude for the healing and help they had received, till one after the other came to "the needle's eye," and found that to pass through it they must leave behind something to which they clung. But, even after parting from Mrs. Glover, most of them still claimed to be Christian Scientists, and so added to their teacher's difficulties by spreading abroad false impressions as to what she taught. These misconceptions made it all the more necessary that a textbook of Christian Science should be written, and strengthened her conviction that she should undertake this great work. Thus the next two and a half years were spent in writing "Science and Health." The difficulties which she encountered in these years might well have forced a brave heart to give up the attempt in despair, but possessed with the conviction that it was God's will that this book should be given to the world, nothing could daunt her.

Her childhood had been spent in a home where hard work was the order of the day, and she herself possessed an extraordinary capacity for work which she retained to the end of her life. At eighty-six years of age, she still rose at six in summer and at seven in winter, and spent the whole day in business and study, with the exception of a brief period allotted to a daily drive. In her Message to The Mother Church for 1900 (p. 2), she says, "The song of Christian Science is, 'Work — work — work — watch and pray.'" In her writings she insisted on the importance of working, of improving the moments, of earning money and spending it for the good of the race. Of all forms of work she taught that the highest consists in the constant endeavour to think rightly, to accept no thoughts but those which proceed from God, and thus help mankind to escape from the bondage of sin, fear and illness engendered by false beliefs in the actuality and power of evil.

During the years in which she was writing "Science and Health," Mrs. Glover taught but one class. Her students were constantly pressing themselves on her attention, calling for her assistance in their difficulties, bringing her all their troubles instead of turning for guidance to God, as she was always teaching them to do. As of old they found it easier to consult a person whom they could see, than to rely on the unseen Principle of the universe. Much time was occupied in this way. Besides this teaching work, Mrs. Glover was healing patients, and in the third year preaching and conducting services in a small hall rented for this purpose by some of her students. Her literary work, too, was greatly impeded by the fact that she spent the greater part of these years in boarding houses with people with whom she had little or nothing in common, subjected to much criticism and petty annoyance, and at times to positive persecution. Even after she had saved enough money to buy a little house of her own, she had to be contented with a tiny study-bedroom in the attic, lit only by a skylight, for her means were so limited that she was obliged to let all the rooms but two, this attic study-bedroom and a sitting room where she could receive students, patients and enquirers. Even in this humble little retreat she was not free from rudeness and insult. Thirty years later she told Mr. Arthur Brisbane, of the *Cosmopolitan*, that stones were thrown through her windows.

At last the textbook of Christian Science was

finished. Feeling that the appropriate name would be revealed, Mrs. Glover waited patiently for six weeks, when, lying awake one starry night, the title "Science and Health" came gently to her consciousness. She rose at once and wrote down the name. Six months later one of her students brought her a copy of Wyclif's translation of the New Testament, and pointed out that he uses the words "science and health" where the Authorized Version employs "knowledge of salvation." (See Luke 1:77.)

The first edition of "Science and Health" came out in the autumn of 1875, some of Mrs. Glover's students advancing money to pay for its publication, but great difficulties attended the sale of the book. It was spoiled by misprints, and those to whom the business had been entrusted mismanaged it. Dismayed by nothing, however, Mrs. Glover continued her preparations for a second, revised edition, but her literary work had still to be carried on under the most trying conditions.

CHAPTER VI

IN speaking of the desertion of Mrs. Glover by some of her early followers, the term animal magnetism occasionally is used and it seems desirable to give some idea of how Christian Science regards this subject. Animal magnetism is another name for mesmerism or hypnotism, and these words, used in the broadest sense, designate the supposed activity of the mortal or carnal mind. In their more particular meaning they designate the belief in the supposed influence or control exercised consciously or unconsciously by one human mind over another. It will at once be seen that Mrs. Eddy's great discovery that there is only one Mind, God, the ever-present, omnipotent Mind which is unchanging good, unchanging Love, unchanging Truth, cuts at the very root of this belief. Since God is infinite then there is no place in which evil of any sort can operate. The truth is beautifully stated in Science and Health (p. 171), "Mind's control over the universe, including man, is no longer an open question, but is demonstrable Science." That these so-called forces may be used with humane intention has already been shown in the case of Quimby, but the unsatisfactory result of his treatment has also been shown. Nothing founded on delusion can be satisfactory or desirable, and there is no room in infinite good for any lesser power.

Although mesmerism had long been practised in the Orient, it was only brought publicly to the attention of Europe by a German doctor, Mesmer, in the year 1775. At first it was only employed as a remedial agency, or for the entertainment of the public, but later ill-disposed people began to find that they could make use of it to further their own ambitions and interfere with others. Mrs. Glover began to perceive that some influence appeared to be hindering the progress of Christian Science and causing troubles to her students. Gradually the workings of this supposed power were revealed to her, and she found herself unwillingly obliged to add a chapter on this subject to Science and Health.

There were days in which Moloch appeared to be a great and terrible power; so powerful that men and women felt compelled to sacrifice even their children to appease his destructive wrath. To-day we know that there never was such a being or power. God is Love and God is infinite, therefore Love is infinite; and if Love is infinite there can be no place for animal magnetism or evil to fill, no place in which any evil can operate. Thus it cannot be real in the full meaning of the word. To see this to some extent is to become partly immune from its seeming influence, so Christian Science teaches; to be convinced absolutely of the infinity of God's love, to know this in the inmost recesses of the heart, would mean complete freedom, and that abiding sense of peace which the world can neither give nor take away. Love, God's love reflected, it declares, is the only force which can destroy evil, but before evil can be destroyed it must first be recognized as evil. On this Mrs. Eddy insisted again and again in her writings. No one who is indulging in sin can see sin's unreality. As our sense of purity increases, our sense of evil will decrease till the kingdom of heaven is fully established within us.

Ignorance is no protection, Mrs. Eddy affirmed. At first she herself did not understand how animal magnetism works, and shrank from investigating its modes and methods; but gradually she came to see the necessity of this action. Some new factor was present, hindering the progress of her work, making the healing more difficult, and causing difficulties between the students. Thus it came to pass that she was led to uncover and disclose the secret workings of this so-called force, and to show her followers how to defend themselves and others from its seeming power. Those who obeyed her instructions and constantly sought for divine guidance and help learned much from their experiences, but there were others who were unwilling to purify their thoughts sufficiently to rise above this belief in evil, and who therefore came under its influence, fell away from Christian Science and joined the ranks of its opponents.

It is hardly necessary to say that these people became the worst opponents of the cause which they had once so enthusiastically supported, but in spite of their plans and efforts, Christian Science was constantly gaining ground.

Stormy and difficult as were the times through which she was passing, it was at this period that great happiness came into Mrs. Glover's life. Amongst those who came to her for healing was a certain Asa Gilbert Eddy. After recovering his health, he went through one of Mrs. Glover's classes, and became an ardent and devoted Christian Scientist. He was the first of the students to announce himself to the world as a Christian Scientist and to place these words on his office sign. On New Year's day, 1877, Mary Glover and he were married at Lynn by the minister whose services she had formerly attended. Of this marriage Mrs. Eddy wrote in "Retrospection and Introspection" (p. 42) that it was a "blessed and spiritual union." At last she had found another prepared to give all his time, energy and capacity to forward the spread and establishment of Christian Science, a devoted husband, a true companion and friend.

He was the youngest son of his parents, and had been the stay of their old age; in gratitude for his loving care they had left him their farm in Vermont, but at the time when he met Mrs. Glover he was engaged in business in East Boston.

The family from which he sprang traced its

descent to a Vicar of Cranbrook, Kent, who had been in his time an undergraduate of Trinity College, Cambridge, and had taken his B. A. degree in 1583. Two of the vicar's sons and one of his daughters left England in 1630 to join the great Puritan Movement, and help to found a new country in a new world where they would be free to worship God according to the dictates of their conscience.

Shortly before her marriage, Mrs. Eddy founded an association which she named the Christian Scientist Association. She had come to see the desirability of an organization which should hold her students together and act as a defence to preserve Christian Science pure and unsullied. It was a very small affair in the beginning, consisting only of Mrs. Eddy and six of her students, but it was the first step towards the foundation of a church. This followed in the course of three years. Although Mr. and Mrs. Eddy were still living in Lynn, she saw that the "Church of Christ, Scientist," must be founded in Boston. This accordingly was accomplished and a charter received from the State. Her students invited Mrs. Eddy to become their pastor; she accepted the call, and was ordained in 1881.

At first services were held in private houses; then for a short time in a public hall. In 1883, they began to be held regularly in the now demolished Hawthorne Hall, Park Street, Boston.

Another organization which she founded about

this time was the Massachusetts Metaphysical College. She obtained a college charter in 1881, which enabled the college to confer regular valid degrees. It was the only institution ever incorporated for the teaching of metaphysics only, as in the following year the Act under which it was incorporated was repealed, and during the intervening twelve months no application was made on behalf of any other metaphysical college.

How did Mrs. Eddy regard organization?

As a highly important means to an end, but not as an object in itself. She declared that the spirit of Christianity is far more important than the form, and that the time will come when the Church of Christ shall be so established in the hearts of men that there will be no need of organization through which to manifest it; but her constant endeavour was to find new channels through which the healing waters of Christian Science might spread over the face of the world, and she regarded organization as a pressing need.

In the Christian Scientist Association, the National Christian Scientist Association and the Church of 1879, the constitution and by-laws were formed by Mrs. Eddy and adopted by her followers. In the case of the Church organized in 1892, "The First Church of Christ, Scientist," or "The Mother Church," the By-Laws in the Church Manual were formed by her and adopted first by the Directors and First Members and later by the Directors only.

She tells us in "Miscellaneous Writings" (p. 148) that the By-Laws presented themselves to her thought at different dates, and as the need for them was unfolded, that "They were impelled by a power not one's own, were written at different dates, and as the occasion required," and in another place she wrote that they were "the fruit of experience and the result of prayer" (Miscellany, p. 343). They were not personal commands laid by her on her followers. We have already seen that Christian Science teaches that by looking to Principle, the governing law of the universe, we can become as conscious to-day as were the saints and heroes of old of the divine guidance, and can therefore be supplied with wisdom and foresight in every right transaction of our life. Thus Christian Scientists regard the Manual of The Mother Church, The First Church of Christ, Scientist, the volume which contains the Church By-Laws, as a divinely inspired guide, a chart by which they can safely navigate the stormy waters of human experience. Their gratitude to Mrs. Eddy for the Manual and for all her other works is gratitude that one was found humble and selfless enough to perceive the divine guidance, and sufficiently loving to give what she had perceived to the world, for the benefit of the world, yet in the face of its constant opposition.

The Metaphysical College proved a great success, for in Boston Mrs. Eddy found a more receptive frame of mind, and more cultivated supporters. Soon students flocked to the College from all over the United States, and later on even from Europe. Mrs. Eddy had from the first been its President, and taught nearly all the classes, since the students naturally felt that they would derive more benefit from her instruction than from that of her students. She was, however, assisted in the work by her husband, who taught for two terms, and by two other of her students in a lesser degree, but at the end of nine years she decided to close the College. It was impossible for her longer to cope with the numbers who desired to enter, and who would be contented with no other teacher; fresh needs were making themselves felt, especially the need for revising the textbook, now renamed "Science and Health with Key to the Scriptures," and she dreaded the very success of the institution. It had accomplished a great work for Christian Science, sending out teachers and practitioners to all parts of the country. Thus alike indifferent to the appeals of ambition and popularity, and to those of wealth, she put the desirability of closing the College before those of her students who acted as directors, and they, by a unanimous vote, decided to follow her advice and dissolve the institution.

In like manner, she advised the dissolution of the National Christian Scientist Association when she felt that its period of usefulness had passed, pointing out that the time spent yearly in preparing for its conventions could be much better employed in the individual effort to rise to a higher spiritual level, and so gain confidence and increased power in healing and teaching. Several years earlier she had recommended all Christian Science teachers to form associations of their own students, so as to guide their footsteps till they should be fit to sustain themselves.

We are here reminded of Tennyson's words:

"The old order changeth, yielding place to new;
And God fulfils Himself in many ways,
Lest one good custom should corrupt the world."

(The Passing of Arthur)

How many institutions which were once in the van of progress have become in the course of time a hindrance to further reform!

Mr. and Mrs. Eddy left Lynn finally in the year 1882, and took a trip to Washington, where they went thoroughly into the question of copyrights, a step which was of the greatest importance to Christian Science. After several months, they returned to Boston, and took an unfurnished house in Columbus Avenue, then one of the pleasant residential streets in the city.

A Mr. E. J. Arens in Boston had produced a pamphlet on mental healing, of which thirty pages were entirely taken from Science and Health. In his preface he stated that he had made use of "some thoughts contained in a book by Eddy." An action was brought against him for infringement of copyright, and a writ of injunction from the United States Circuit Court in Boston was issued, and the pamphlet destroyed. His defence was that the copyrighted works of Mrs. Eddy were really taken by her from manuscripts of P. P. Quimby, but no evidence to prove this statement was brought forward. His counsel being asked why this evidence had not been produced, simply replied that there was no evidence to present. From this it was naturally supposed by many that no such MSS. existed, and the matter remained a mystery till in 1921 the widow of Dr. Quimby's son George gave Horatio Dresser permission to publish all the writings of her late father-in-law. The papers handed over consisted partly of writings and short essays in Quimby's own hand, and partly in other writings of a similar nature copied out under his directions by his son George and two ladies who were his friends and followers. There were also letters from Quimby to his patients, and from patients to him.

Mr. Dresser contends that the volume will prove that Christian Science was largely taken from Quimby's writings, instead of being the revelation Mrs. Eddy declared it to be. On page 436 of his book he quotes from a letter written by George Quimby in 1901, in which he says: "As far as the book 'Science and Health,' is concerned, Mrs. Eddy had no access to father's MSS. [save 'Questions and Answers'] when she wrote it, but that she did have a very full knowledge of his ideas and beliefs is also true. The *religion* which she teaches certainly *is hers*, for which I cannot be too thankful; for I should be loath to go down to my grave feeling that my father was in any way connected with 'Christian Science.' . . . In curing the sick [conventional] religion played no part. There were no prayers, there was no asking assistance from God or any other divinity."

But he declared that Mrs. Eddy had taken from his father the idea that illness is a mental condition and is an invention of man. To this assertion we must point out that Dr. Quimby was by no means the first who taught the mental cause of disease, and that, moreover, Mrs. Eddy had been convinced of this fact long before she sought his assistance. Besides this, though he believed that illness originated in the patient's mind, he did not hold that illness itself is mental, as is shown by his use of manipulation. The quotations following plainly illustrate the divergence between his views and those of Christian Science. To a patient in 1860 he writes: "Of course you get very tired, and this would cause the heat to affect the surface as your head was affected, the heat would affect the fluids, and when the heat came in contact with the cold it would chill the surface" (Quimby Manuscripts, p. 113).

To another he describes his method of giving an absent treatment. "Your letter apprised me of your situation, and I went to see if I could affect you. . . .

So I will sit by you a short time and relieve the pain in your stomach and carry it off. . . . Sit up straight. I am now rubbing the back part of your head and round the roots of your nose. I do not know as you feel my hand . . . but it will make you feel better. . . . I am in this letter, so remember and look at me . . ." (Quimby Manuscripts, p. 111).

On page 12, Mr. Dresser says of Quimby: "This same practice led to his view of matter and the natural world in general as a subordinate expression of Spirit." As against this, Christian Science teaches that matter is simply a false impression, uncreated by and therefore unknown to Spirit, and possessing no more substance or reality than the matter which confronts us in the dream of the night.

On page 348, Quimby declares that the character of the teacher cannot affect the science which he teaches; "it is not absolutely necessary that he should be a good man or a bad man." To some extent all will admit this as applied to the sciences and arts of this world. A non-Christian or a man of low moral standard might be proficient in some branch of natural science, a skilful surgeon or an accomplished musician, but he could not be a true exponent of the Science of Christianity. Quimby was himself a kind, honourable, upright man, but the fact that he could entertain such an opinion as above quoted plainly proves that his healing was not spiritual, was not the direct action of the Holy Spirit.

[86]

Christian Science is a complete whole; its theology is absolutely essential to the healing; the healing is the visible manifestation of the theology. It makes, and can make, no compromise with matter. It must be accepted in its entirety or not accepted at all.

It is worthy of notice that none of Dr. Quimby's patients and followers carried on his healing work from the time of his death in 1866. Julius Dresser, father of the editor of the book above referred to, who was a patient and intimate friend of Quimby's, stated in a letter which he wrote to Mrs. Patterson just after the doctor passed away, that he did not know nor did he believe anyone living knew how Dr. Quimby healed the sick, and that he himself had been unable to heal his wife of a slight ailment. It was not till 1883 that his son made the charge that Mrs. Eddy had taken her main ideas from Quimby, and that Christian Science is only an offshoot of his teachings.

We have already seen that Mr. and Mrs. Eddy left Lynn in 1882, and shortly thereafter settled in Boston, but their happy companionship was soon to be broken. Mr. Eddy's health gave way under the ceaseless attacks made upon him and his wife, culminating in the recent attempt to infringe her copyright and to adulterate Christian Science. In his unselfish love for his wife, and the cause of Christian Science, he represented himself as less ill than he was, and thus refused to avail himself fully of her services, that she might be free to attend to the pressing calls of the hour.

He passed away in June of that year "with a smile of peace and love resting on his serene countenance" (Retrospection and Introspection, p. 42), and once more Mrs. Eddy was left to face the storms of opposition alone. She met this great sorrow with her usual heroism. She had a hard struggle to rise above the sense of grief and loneliness, but she gained the victory.

How does Christian Science regard death?

It regards it as part of the belief in material life, and therefore as unreal in the strict meaning of the word. It has already been shown that Christian Science teaches that the real nature or essence of man is immortal, since man is the outcome or reflection of God, the immortal. Thus it declares that there can be but one kind of life, and that mental or spiritual. All belief in living or dying in matter, it contends, is but a dream, as unreal as the dreams we have in sleep, and a dream has never affected, and can never affect, the real nature of man. Moreover, it affirms, we awaken from this dream of material life and death solely in proportion to our understanding and manifestation of the nature of God. As our thoughts become more God-like, we shall depend less and less on matter, and consequently believe less in it, till we prove the truth of our Lord's statement: "I am the resurrection, and the life: he that believeth in me, though he were dead, yet shall he live: and whosoever liveth and believeth in me shall never die" (John 11:25, 26).

Christian Science also teaches that those who have passed through the experience called death in no wise lose their individuality, for this is a necessary characteristic of every idea of the divine Mind. Moreover, it declares that they find themselves with "bodies unseen by those who think that they bury the body" (Science and Health, p. 429), since the material body, so-called, is the expression or outward manifestation of material thought, and mortal thought is not destroyed by death, but by spiritual growth. Those, then, who have made good use of their time here and have been increasing in spirituality waken to a fuller and truer sense of life, and need not experience a second death, whilst those whose affections and interests have been centred on the material, will find that they have but entered on a fresh dream of material living and dying.

Thus it maintains that there is "a probationary and progressive state beyond the grave" (Science and Health, p. 46), but that eventually every prodigal will find his way home, every wandering sheep find the fold, and man be satisfied, when he awakes from these dreams, with God's likeness.

CHAPTER VII

THE next step which presented itself to Mrs. Eddy was the starting of a Christian Science periodical, which appeared for the first time in April, 1883. It was called the *Journal of Christian Science*, a title which was soon changed for that of *The Christian Science Journal*. Mrs. Eddy was its first publisher and editor. It had its inception in Mrs. Eddy's thought, and the Christian Scientist Association lent support to its establishment. For many years, Mrs. Eddy was its chief contributor, and many of the articles which she wrote for it are now collected together in "Miscellaneous Writings."

By means of this monthly magazine she was able to reach a larger public, to answer the questions and explain the difficulties of a wider circle of enquirers, to show clearly the difference between Christian Science and other systems not based on the absolute supremacy of God, and to counteract the fear of disease inspired by the descriptions of illnesses with which the newspapers of the day were loaded. It was "designed to bring health and happiness to all households wherein it is permitted to enter, and to confer increased power to be good and to do good" (Miscellaneous Writings, p. 262).

Although Mrs. Eddy wrote many articles herself for *The Christian Science Journal*, she held before her students the duty which lay on them of contributing their share. She reminded them of the large number of eager readers who were looking to the *Journal* for help and comfort, and urged them to give their assistance in this important work. She deprecated all personal attacks upon those opposed to Christian Science and maintained the necessity for impartiality, courteousness, charity and humility in all dealings with our fellow men. In the Manual (p. 48) will be found the following By-Law: "A member of this Church shall not publish, nor cause to be published, an article that is uncharitable or impertinent towards religion, medicine, the courts, or the laws of our land."

Six years from its start, *The Christian Science Journal* was in a flourishing condition, so Mrs. Eddy presented it and the profits accruing therefrom to the National Christian Scientist Association. After this association was dissolved it eventually became the property of The Christian Science Publishing Society, the net profits being handed over to the Treasurer of The Mother Church. It remained the only organ of the church until 1890 when the *Christian Science Quarterly* was published. Then in 1898 a weekly periodical eventually called the *Christian Science Sentinel* was also started by Mrs. Eddy. It became a medium through which Mrs. Eddy and the Church officials communicated with the members of the Church. Both the *Journal* and the *Sentinel* contain articles on Christian Science and testimonies from those who have been reformed, healed or helped in other ways by the study of Christian Science or by Christian Science treatment.

The fourth periodical to appear was printed in German and was called *The Herald of Christian Science*. It was "to proclaim the universal activity and availability of Truth" (Miscellany, p. 353). This monthly magazine is now printed with articles and testimonies in German on one page, with the English text opposite. In this way German readers become acquainted with English, and so may learn to read the Christian Science books in the original.*

In 1908, Mrs. Eddy directed the taking of another great forward step. On November 25, a daily newspaper made its appearance from The Christian Science Publishing Society, which she had named *The Christian Science Monitor*. She had long felt the need of such a paper, a paper which should take its place amongst the leading newspapers of the world, whilst upholding a higher standard than any yet attained.

Of this paper Mrs. Eddy wrote, "The object of the *Monitor* is to injure no man, but to bless all man-

---

*Since the inauguration of the German Edition, *The Herald of Christian Science* has been issued in various language editions. Today, in response to a demonstrated need, The Christian Science Publishing Society publishes the *Herald* in a wide variety of languages, as well as in Braille.

kind" (Miscellany, p. 353). Thus the *Monitor* in maintaining this high standard is endeavouring to keep its readers correctly informed as to the trend of events that they may think rightly regarding human welfare and progress, and so, rising above ignorance and prejudice, help to bring about changes which make for the common good of mankind and a better understanding between the nations.

It need hardly be said that Mrs. Eddy was a strong advocate of international conciliation. She taught that in proportion as men kept the First Commandment, and recognized God as the one and only Mind would they be able to understand the brotherhood of man. That meanwhile difficulties between nations can rightly be solved by wise, just arbitration. In 1908 she wrote that at that date navies were undoubtedly required to prevent war and preserve the peace of the world.

Mrs. Eddy was a thoroughly patriotic American, and appreciated patriotism in people of other countries. She believed firmly in the Constitution of the United States, and constantly emphasized the necessity of obeying the laws. Thus she enjoined on her followers the propriety of submitting to vaccination when this is a legal requirement, and the duty of having cases of contagion reported to the proper authorities when the law so requires.

We have already seen that the first Church of Christ (Scientist) was organized in 1879, and its charter obtained from the State of Massachusetts. It was named the "Church of Christ, Scientist," and it was to be a church without creeds, and was designed, as we learn from the Manual (p. 17), "to commemorate the word and works of our Master" and to "reinstate primitive Christianity and its lost element of healing."

In 1889, on Mrs. Eddy's advice, the members resolved unanimously to dissolve this Church. Nevertheless it continued to function as a voluntary association until The Mother Church, The First Church of Christ, Scientist, in Boston, Massachusetts, was organized, on September 23, 1892. The continuity of purpose of her former Church, however, remained unbroken.

At the time of the organization of this Church, its Tenets, Rules and By-Laws were adopted, and three years later a further step was taken when personal preaching was abolished and the Bible and Science and Health were ordained as Pastor. This new order came into effect on the day on which The Mother Church edifice was dedicated. Before that date the successive pastors of the Church had preached excellent sermons which had been greatly appreciated by the congregation, but Mrs. Eddy foresaw the dangers which attach themselves to preaching, amongst these being the gradual substitution of personal views and opinions for the absolute truth in the Bible and her writings.

The Lesson-Sermons, which consist entirely of passages from the Bible and Science and Health, are prepared by a committee which devotes much time and thought to this important work. The subjects of these sermons were fixed by Mrs. Eddy, and are used twice in the course of the year, but they are treated in various ways, so that there is no monotony in this arrangement. The Lesson-Sermon is the most distinctive feature in the Sunday services; it is read by the First and Second Readers, one of whom, in The Mother Church, shall be a man and the other a woman. In Christian Science there is not the usual distinction made between sacred and secular callings. There is no priesthood, and every faithful member of the Church who has the necessary qualifications for such an office is eligible as Reader.

In the same way, every Christian Scientist should be able to heal the sick, though only those who are able to devote all their time to this work can have their names entered as Christian Science practitioners in the official directory, which appears at the end of *The Christian Science Journal.*

In addition to the Sunday services, a meeting is held in each church on Wednesday evening. It is conducted by the First Reader and consists of readings from the Bible and from Science and Health, hymns, silent prayer, the Lord's Prayer, in which the congregation joins, and testimonies of healing from the congregation. The readings and hymns are selected by the First Reader, and chosen so as to bring out one central idea. About half of the hour allotted to the meeting is occupied with the testimonies as to the benefits the speakers have received from the study of Christian Science and from treatment. This part of the meeting is in no way arranged beforehand; it is left to each individual's judgment to speak or to keep silent. In some of the larger churches each speaker is limited to three minutes, as there are so many anxious to express their gratitude and to cheer and encourage others by the recital of their own experiences.

Christian Scientists visiting a town on business or for pleasure make a point of attending the Wednesday meeting, and the good news they bring from other fields, and often from other continents, greatly adds to the interest of the occasion.

The Christian Science churches throughout the world are known as branch churches, and each branch church is self-governed. Each forms its own rules and by-laws in conformity with the Manual of The Mother Church, and elects its own Directors, Readers and other officials in the manner that seems most appropriate to the locality; there is, however, a proviso in the Manual that all Readers must be members of The Mother Church, and thus amenable to its rules.

The order of services, of course, is the same in The Mother Church and in its branch churches, and the same Lesson-Sermon from the *Christian Science*

Quarterly is read on Sundays in every Christian Science service throughout the world.

Silent prayer is another distinctive feature of the Christian Science service. The only audible prayer used is the "Lord's Prayer," with its spiritual interpretation as given on pages 16 and 17 of Science and Health.

Christian Science reiterates the apostolic injunctions, "Rejoice evermore. Pray without ceasing. In every thing give thanks" (I Thessalonians 5:16–18), and declares that true prayer is an attitude of mind, a profound desire to express the nature of God, a constant endeavour to rise above apathy, selfishness, worldliness and sin of all sorts. It is a constant song of gratitude to God for being God, unchanging Truth, unfailing Love, unending Life.

If our prayers remain unanswered, then it is for us to ask ourselves, "Why so?" God is the fundamental governing law of the universe, "the Father of lights, with whom is no variableness, neither shadow of turning," therefore we cannot expect to change His nature or His mode of action. The benefit derived from prayer is in the proportion that it brings us into closer communion with Him. The more we dwell on our unity with God as God's reflection, possessing no Mind but that which was in Christ, the less shall we believe in and fear the supposed power of sin, disease and death, the sooner will mere faith in God grow into spiritual understanding of Him.

[97]

Christian Science deprecates audible prayer in public because it often leads men into hypocrisy, uttering with the lips that to which the heart does not reply "Amen." Praying to be better is no substitute for reformation. The proof of true prayer is shown forth in a humbler, juster, more generous outlook on life, in deeds of unselfishness and kindness to our brother man.

Christian Science shows that sin punishes itself, that, therefore, as we get rid of sin we get rid of the suffering it brings, but as long as we sin we must suffer. Prayer cannot change this great fact. It also shows us that the constant declaration that we are miserable sinners no more helps us to part company with sin than the constant declaration that we always make mistakes in arithmetic would help us to become mathematicians. We need to know what is true concerning the nature of God and man and strive to live in accordance with this truth.

It has been stated that the Church of Christ, Scientist, is without creeds, and was formed to "reinstate primitive Christianity and its lost element of healing" (Manual, p. 17). The healing of Christian Science can no more be accomplished by mere belief in God than can mathematical problems be solved by mere belief in mathematics. In each case a scientific understanding of the subject is required. The greatest value of the so-called physical healing effected by Christian Science consists in the proof it affords of the nature and relationship of God and man, of the presence and tenderness and availability of the heavenly Father.

As we all know, the word "creed" is taken from the Latin "credo," "I believe" — the first word in the creed we call "The Apostles' Creed." This creed and the Nicene are the two most ancient of the creeds, but in their present form they only date from the fifth century A. D. Thus it will be seen that they belong to a period far later than the Apostolic age, to a period when the healing of primitive Christianity had become lost to the world. Christian Science, therefore, does not look for enlightenment to the interpretation placed on the Gospel statements by ages which had lost the power to heal, since this inability, it affirms, could but proceed from a lack of understanding of the Master's teachings.

There is nothing mysterious in God, nothing mysterious in the words of our Lord. "I thank thee, O Father, Lord of heaven and earth, that thou hast hid these things from the wise and prudent, and hast revealed them unto babes" (Matthew 11:25).

As men divest themselves of pride, prejudice and unwillingness to learn, things which seemed mysteries to the worldly mind become plain, as when the bright veil of day is withdrawn, we become conscious of the immensity and beauty of the starry heavens.

With the student of Christian Science, in proportion as he understands our Lord's words and works does he find himself capable of healing; and as the capacity to heal himself and others increases, his capacity to understand our Lord's words and works increases more and more. The divinity of Christ and the inspiration of the Holy Ghost become to him, not merely articles of faith, but living realities, indisputable facts.

Christian Science accepts the Gospel narrative as a true record of events. It accepts as actual facts the virgin birth, the resurrection and ascension, but it does not regard them as miraculous occurrences. It holds them to be manifestations of spiritual law which eventually will be understood by all. It regards Jesus Christ as the Saviour of the world: "No man cometh unto the Father, but by me"; but it also points to his words spoken to the lawyer: "Why callest thou me good? none is good, save one, that is, God," and to the words of St. Luke (2:52), "And Jesus increased in wisdom and stature, and in favour with God and man." These seemingly contradictory statements are made plain by the teaching of Christian Science. It recognizes that the person of the dear Master partook of human limitations, though in an immeasurably less degree than that of any other, and that it was not the personality but the Mind which was in Christ Jesus which was divine, and which saved the world.

We may here say a few words about the view which Christian Science takes of communion and baptism. We are all aware that in only one of the four Gospels — that of St. Luke — is anything said of the perpetuation of the Lord's Supper, but there is also an account of this institution in the 11th chapter of 1st Corinthians.

St. Luke's Gospel, according to Westcott, was written a little later than the first Epistle to the Corinthians. Thus the account given in Corinthians is the earliest as well as the fullest of the accounts. It is perhaps worth noting here that neither St. Luke nor St. Paul was present at the original Supper.

In the 26th verse of the 11th chapter we read: "For as often as ye eat this bread, and drink this cup, ye do shew the Lord's death till he come."

In the 14th chapter of St. John's Gospel, our Lord speaks of what is generally known as his "Second Coming," but these verses plainly show that this second coming, or the advent of the spirit of Truth, was a coming to the individual heart of man. This is the light in which Christian Science regards it. When anyone has become really and intimately conscious, through actual demonstration, of the presence of the healing Christ, he can no longer show forth the Lord's death, because for him the Christ has come again; he has perceived the risen Saviour. The communion, therefore, which Christian Scientists hold, commemorates the morning meal which our Lord prepared for his disciples, on the shores of the Lake of Galilee, during those wonderful forty days between the resurrection and the ascension. Their thought is centred on his victory over death, on the triumph of love over hate.

No material symbols are used, as Mrs. Eddy was convinced that rites and ceremonies lead men to depend upon the outward and material, instead of on the reformation of the heart, the transformation of the mind.

In like manner, the rites of circumcision and of the Passover which were regarded by the Jews as of God's appointing gave way to the more spiritual forms connected with the holy communion and baptism. So the material rites pertaining to these in their turn will pass, as a higher and more spiritual understanding of worship asserts itself in the consciousness of men. "God is a spirit: and they that worship him must worship him in spirit and in truth" (John 4:24).

From what has been said concerning communion, it will not seem surprising that the Church Manual does not make provision for a baptismal service.

Baptism, according to Christian Science, is nothing less than "a purification from all error" (Science and Health, p. 35). It is not, therefore, a brief ceremony to be performed; it is an object to the attainment of which the whole energy of man must be devoted. It means a complete change of the outlook on life, a revolution of thought, regeneration. No infant has undergone this process, nor can undergo it, thus the only effect that baptism can produce is on older people, including those who have brought the child to be baptized. If the ceremony leads them to think more seriously of their duty to the little one, then it is helpful; but if it only brings a sense that something has been accomplished, then it becomes a positive hindrance.

Christian Science lays great stress on the importance of teaching children from the earliest possible age the great facts which it has to present, that they may learn to love God, to recognize Him as an ever-present help in time of trouble; that they may learn how to resist evil and suggestions of ill-health, through knowing that they are not sent by Love, and are therefore unreal.

It urges on parents the great importance of keeping the mental atmosphere which surrounds their children pure, of insisting on obedience to God's laws, and so aiding their growth in self-control. It points out that the fears and health-beliefs entertained about their children by parents and guardians may tend to produce the very ills which they dread to see manifested.

The Sunday School forms an integral part of the Church of Christ, Scientist, and is generally well attended because — strange as this may seem to one unacquainted with this Science — it appeals to the children themselves, and they soon find themselves able to demonstrate Christian Science in many ways. No Sunday School treats or entertainments are given, nor are any prizes awarded, so that it is a real interest in the lessons which attracts, and nothing else.

On the temperance question Christian Science takes up a strong position. It declares emphatically against the use of all intoxicating liquors, and against the use of tobacco, but it maintains that men need to be cured of these tastes, freed from these forms of bondage, just as much as from illness. It is not by condemnation that people are raised to a higher level, but by becoming conscious of the satisfaction of Spirit, the infinite tenderness of God. The treatment of the Christian Science practitioner opens the window of the darkened sense, and lets in the pure air and sunshine of heaven, and the craving for strong drink fades away.

CHAPTER VIII

THE reader will doubtless wish to hear when Mrs. Eddy met her son George again, and what was the result of this meeting. It was in 1879, after long years of separation, that they saw one another again. He had found out that his mother was alive, and came to see her, but it was a sad experience for her. After a few weeks she saw that they had little in common. She tried to impart to him some sense of spiritual things, of the facts of being as taught by Christian Science, but they made no impression on him and effected no change in his mode of life.

Mrs. Eddy, however, gave him freely what he was able to receive. On his subsequent visit to Boston, in 1888, with his wife and children, she took a house for them, and introduced them to many of her friends, who showed them much hospitality and kindness. After his return to the West, she provided money to build him a house, money to forward his business affairs, money to assist him with the education of his children, and later she made suitable provision by a trust fund for him and his family, but her longing for a son's support and a son's sympathy remained unsatisfied.

In the year following George Glover's second

visit to Boston, the Metaphysical College was closed, and Mrs. Eddy left Boston to take up her abode in Concord, the capital of New Hampshire.

Her financial position had greatly improved in the past ten years, her unremitting toil had lifted her out of poverty into affluence. God had provided for her whilst she was providing for others.

In 1887 Mrs. Eddy bought a house in Commonwealth Avenue, the finest residential street in Boston, and later lent it to the Church for the use of the First Reader for the time being. Now she bought a property in the outskirts of Concord, "Pleasant View," and remodelled the old farmhouse, which stood on the ridge of a hill, into a pretty and modest home. Everything about the place expressed order, brightness, tender care. The handsome horses, the good stables, the coachman's comfortable house, the rose garden, the fishes in the fountain, the bullfrogs in the pond, all things expressed well-being and comfort.

After Mrs. Eddy passed away, the house was removed, but it remains in happy memory, surrounded by green lawns, with the cloudless summer sky above, looking down past a little pond and a pleasant meadow fringed with trees, to the well-wooded valley of the Merrimac. Since then, The Christian Science Pleasant View Home for elderly Christian Scientists has been built in its place.*

*This property was sold in 1975.

If Mrs. Eddy had none of her kith and kin to help her and love her and keep watch over her in her advancing years, she had with her devoted and grateful students — Mrs. Laura Sargent and Mr. Calvin Frye — who were with her, the first for seventeen years, and the second for twenty-eight years. Miss Shannon and many others also came from time to time to help with secretarial and other work and looked upon their time at Pleasant View and their daily contacts with Mrs. Eddy as the most valuable experience of their lives.

For more than twenty years she had given to her students the most intimate and direct guidance, as a wise mother guides her little ones, but now she saw that the time had come when her students must carry on the work on the lines laid down by her, with less supervision, depending less on her and more on God. She longed to retire from the pressure of the life she had been leading, to revise Science and Health, to have time for meditation, to learn more of the life of the Spirit, to be able to see the future steps which must be taken to safeguard and establish the cause of Christian Science. Those of her students who knew her best felt that she was like a grown-up person in a world of children. At times she would try to tell them of the things which were appearing to her mental vision, but they could only follow her a little way. They had not reached the spiritual altitude whence these things could be discerned.

[107]

We read in the Old and New Testaments of many striking instances where prayer, communion with God, bestowed on men wonderful foresight and practical wisdom. Christian Science teaches that this is a scientific and natural fact. It declares that if God is indeed Mind, the only Mind, the solution of every problem with which we can be confronted is to be found by subordinating fear and belief in a self apart from God and looking to God alone. In this way Mrs. Eddy was constantly looking for the divine guidance in the practical affairs of everyday life, and the By-Laws which she brought forward from time to time, and the organization of various new branches of Christian Science activity were, she was convinced, the outcome of her prayers.

The Christian Science movement was growing apace. In the *Journal* for 1899 can be seen a list of Christian Science practitioners, which include many names in Canada and some in England and Scotland, France and Germany. There was even a practitioner in Peking and one in Hawaii. Science and Health, in 1884, was in its ninth edition of a thousand copies each, the 16th came out in the following year, and the 172nd bears the date of 1899. In her Message to The Mother Church for 1900, Mrs. Eddy says that she had for many years desired to hand over the leadership of the movement to others, but had found no one who could take her place. It was no wonder that she begged her followers to refrain from sending her presents, letters and telegrams of congratulation at Christmas, Easter, or other special days, and that she was unable to see many whom otherwise she would have liked to meet, or to accept the invitations which she was constantly receiving to be present at dedication services, exhibitions, etc. She had work to do of which her followers could know nothing, work to do for the whole human race, things to contemplate beyond their ken.

The result of this time of seclusion was soon to be shown openly in new ways and means of spreading Christian Science.

For many years Mrs. Eddy had been looking forward to the time when The First Church of Christ, Scientist, should possess a home of its own. Church services were held successively in the private homes of students, Mrs. Eddy's home, Hawthorne Hall, the Massachusetts Metaphysical College building, and finally in public halls in Boston. In 1887–88 a fund was raised with considerable difficulty by the students of Christian Science, but the money was lost. Later more money was collected, and a suitable site found, but as the students could give only a part of the required price, the rest was secured by a mortgage. When this became due they were still unable to pay the full amount, so Mrs. Eddy came forward and bought the lot. She then conveyed it on behalf of the Church to a Board of Trustees. Fresh trouble arose, so Mrs. Eddy again took the land into her own hands, and in September, 1892, she established a Deed of Trust which created The Christian Science Board of Directors and conveyed the land to that Board. The Directors were bound to erect a church building on the ground within the next five years.

We have seen from the above brief sketch the difficulties which had beset the beginning of the undertaking, and Mrs. Eddy foresaw the difficulties which would arise before the building could be finished, but Christian Science had shown her that evil is never person, place nor thing, but only a mesmeric suggestion that God, good, is not omnipotent and the only cause. Thus if anyone sees the omnipotence of good with sufficient clearness and maintains this position in spite of the testimony of the physical senses, evil of every sort must disappear as darkness before dawn. With this conviction she advised the Directors to lay the foundation stone in October, 1893, and to complete the building in 1894. The first stone was actually laid on the 8th of November, 1893, and a communion service held in the finished building on December 30, 1894.

The history of how this was accomplished in the face of difficulties of every sort is not only interesting reading, but is an excellent illustration of the application of Christian Science to business affairs. The account is given in a small book called "The Mother Church," and the author, Mr. Armstrong, was one of the Directors who were responsible for the work.

"One month before the close of the year every evidence of material sense declared that the church's completion within the year 1894 transcended human possibility. The predictions of workman and on-looker alike were that it could not be completed before April or May of 1895. . . . . It has proved, in most striking manner, the oft-repeated declarations of our textbooks, that the evidence of the mortal senses is unreliable" (Pulpit and Press, p. 45).

The church is built of light grey Concord granite — a very beautiful stone — and has a very handsome Romanesque tower, and all the interior fittings are of the best. It is lit by electricity, and is seated to hold 1100 people.

The required money was raised in fourteen months by the Christian Scientists themselves without the help of bazaars, concerts or entertainments of any sort; and every account was paid by the 6th of January when the church was dedicated. In the January number of *The Christian Science Journal* appeared a notice from the Treasurer thanking the contributors to the Church Building Fund, and requesting that no further donations should be sent in after January 6, 1895, when the fund would be closed.

The years 1898 and 1899 were memorable ones in the history of the Christian Science movement. An important step was taken on January 25, 1898, when Mrs. Eddy created the Deed of Trust establishing the present Christian Science Publishing Society.

According to the provision of the Church Manual, the editors of the periodicals and the business manager of the Publishing Society were to be appointed by the Directors, who were also to see that the periodicals were "ably edited and kept abreast of the times" (Manual, p. 44) — and to provide a suitable building for the publishing business; on the other hand the Trustees of the Publishing Society were to pay over semi-annually to the Church treasurer the net profits of the business, and were to conduct that business "on a strictly Christian basis, for the promotion of the interests of Christian Science" (Manual, p. 80). That year there appeared from the printing presses a new weekly periodical, now named *Christian Science Sentinel*.

The Board of Lectureship was also instituted in 1898. It was followed soon by the first appointments of Committees on Publication. In order to understand the important part which these two new organizations were to play, it is necessary to remember the determined opposition which Christian Science encountered from its very start.

The reader will recall the indignation aroused amongst the doctors and clergy of Westerly, Rhode Island, by a wonderful cure which Mrs. Eddy effected, and how the notices of a second lecture which she proposed to give were torn down, and the halls and churches of the town shut against her. We have also heard how stones were thrown through her windows in Lynn at the time when she was engaged in writing Science and Health.

In one of her Messages to The Mother Church, Mrs. Eddy speaks of the anonymous letters which she received in Boston, threatening to blow up the hall where she preached. In the Message for 1902 (p. 14), she writes, "From the beginning of the great battle every forward step has been met (not by mankind, but by a kind of men) with mockery, envy, rivalry, and falsehood — as achievement after achievement has been blazoned on the forefront of the world and recorded in heaven." The dissemination of false statements through newspapers, pamphlets, lectures and sermons never ceased.

Mrs. Eddy did not regard these attacks as directed simply against herself — though such they appeared to be; she recognized them as attempts on the part of the carnal mind which is "enmity against God" (Rom. 8:7) to stop the currents of truth, to hinder the progress of Christian Science, and to turn from it the sufferer and the sinner who were in sore need of its healing and cleansing ministrations.

She felt, therefore, that it was incumbent on her to refute these calumnies and correct mistakes as to what Christian Science teaches, and this she did by lectures, and by articles and letters to the press. In both these lines she had been very successful; she had addressed very large audiences in New York, Boston and Chicago, receiving great ovations in

Chicago in 1888, and in the following year in New York. The substance of one of these lectures which aroused such enthusiasm is to be found in "Miscellaneous Writings," and is called "Science and the Senses," and there are many addresses by her both in "Miscellaneous Writings" and in "The First Church of Christ, Scientist, and Miscellany." "Christian Science versus Pantheism" is the title of the Message to The Mother Church which Mrs. Eddy wrote in 1898. All of Mrs. Eddy's writings except Science and Health, the Manual and Poems are now available in one volume called Prose Works.

She also wrote often in defence of Christian Science to the papers. A certain number of these "replies" and corrections are to be found reprinted in her books. In Science and Health, the chapter now called "Some Objections Answered" appears in early editions as "Reply to a Clergyman" and in "Miscellaneous Writings" there are several articles of this sort, whilst in "The First Church of Christ, Scientist, and Miscellany" there is a chapter called "Answers to Criticisms."

Now it seemed that in lecture work and in giving answers to the press she could have valuable assistance from her students, and devote herself more entirely to the special work which she alone could undertake, that of guarding and directing the whole movement. Thus it came about that the two new branches of Christian Science activity were organized and started by Mrs. Eddy. In 1898 a new By-Law appeared, setting up a Board of Lectureship, and during that year at different dates eleven lecturers — two of them being women — were appointed to serve on it. The special function of these lecturers is to present the public with some accurate information about the teachings of Christian Science, to show that they are strictly in accord with the teachings of the Gospels, to correct with courage and courtesy any false statement concerning Christian Science which may be current at the time, and "to bear testimony to the facts pertaining to the life" (Manual, p. 93) of Mrs. Eddy.

The lectures proved a great success from the very first, and Mrs. Eddy expressed in very warm terms her satisfaction at the manner in which the lecturers had carried out their duties. She commended their wisdom and kindliness, the loving, impersonal way in which they had corrected false statements without attacking their opponents; she rejoiced that they had withstood the temptations of pride and self-satisfaction, and had returned good for evil.

[Now lectures are given virtually throughout the world — in all fifty of the United States, including Alaska and Hawaii, in Canada, Mexico, Central America, South America, the Islands of the Caribbean, in Bermuda, Great Britain, and Ireland; in Western Europe, Africa, the Middle East, Asia, Australia, and New Zealand. Many lectures on the continent and in other parts of the globe are being delivered in the language of the country. College lectures also are being given in many of these areas.]

The lectures are one of the branches of Christian Science activity especially intended for the outside world, and this missionary work is undertaken with great pleasure by Churches of Christ, Scientist, and societies. The church which invites the lecturer bears the costs, the lecturer's fee, which includes his travelling expenses, the charge for the use of the lecture hall, for advertising, etc.; since the public is invited as the church's guests, careful arrangements are made for their comfort, attention being paid to the lighting, heating and ventilation of the hall, and special seats reserved for elderly or infirm people.

Here some may ask why should Christian Scientists pay so much attention to material well being, whilst asserting that there is no matter? Mrs. Eddy's attitude towards the inventions of the age is very clearly stated. Christian Science had revealed to her that mankind is in bondage to ignorance and its attendant fear. She saw, therefore, that anything which helped to expand thought, to enlarge the outlook, was a step in the right direction. Thus she saw the importance of sound education, the value of those inventions which make for a freer and more convenient mode of life, which lift man above mere drudgery, and give him a greater sense of command.

It was in Concord, New Hampshire, in 1898

that Mrs. Eddy taught her last class. Students came from all parts of the United States, from Canada, England, and Scotland, at her invitation. They assembled in Christian Science Hall on Sunday afternoon, November 20, where an explanatory message from Mrs. Eddy was read to them. Then Mrs. Eddy took her place on the platform and began to teach. At the close of the class, these students went away with hearts filled to overflowing, their lives rededicated to the purpose of bringing the revelation of Truth to all who were ready to receive it.

In January, 1900, Mr. Alfred Farlow was summoned from Kansas City, Missouri, to fill the new post of Committee on Publication for The Mother Church. He threw himself with great energy into the work, and soon assistant Committees were appointed in various localities, and general lines laid down to guide them in replying to attacks, and clearing up misrepresentations.

The chief duties of these Committees are thus laid down in the Manual: "to correct in a Christian manner impositions on the public in regard to Christian Science, injustices done Mrs. Eddy or members of this Church by the daily press, by periodicals or circulated literature of any sort" (Manual, p. 97). The work of the Committees has been of much value to the cause of Christian Science. It has led the press to treat this subject with much more respect, and has greatly enlightened the public mind.

The year 1898 witnessed the establishment of the Board of Education as an auxiliary to The Mother Church, and its first class was held in January, 1899. It will be remembered that Mrs. Eddy had closed the Metaphysical College in 1889, and had retired to Concord to have leisure to work out various problems which concerned the advancement of the cause of Christian Science. Amongst these was the subject of teaching. As she was engaged in revising her text-book, the plan to be pursued presented itself to her and developed into the Board of Education. As happened often in her experience, she had received a spiritual intuition, and faithfully obeying, saw later the meaning of the command.

Mrs. Eddy had retained her charter of the Massachusetts Metaphysical College, but she now arranged that the work of preparing Christian Science teachers be carried on by the newly-appointed Board of Education.

The Board of Education is composed of three members, a president, vice-president and teacher, Mrs. Eddy herself being its first president. The duty of this board is to provide for a normal class of thirty students held once in three years, The Christian Science Board of Directors appointing each time the teacher who is to hold the class. Sometimes a man is appointed, sometimes a woman, and the students do not know till the session opens who their teacher is to be.

[118]

Christian Science teaches that to be spiritually minded is, in the highest sense of that word, to be scientifically minded, to think aright. To be spiritually minded means to reflect or express God's nature, to manifest intelligence, capacity, practical ability, as well as those qualities always recognized as spiritual, such as purity, truthfulness, loving kindness. Mrs. Eddy united these qualities in a very remarkable degree, and this enabled her to be both the Discoverer of Christian Science and its Founder. The passing years saw her always progressing, perceiving more, foreseeing more clearly. Nothing seemed to escape her notice, or pass her by without yielding up its lesson. Thus she constantly profited by the experiences of the past. In the affairs of the Church, as in her private affairs, she saw the importance of careful attention to detail. Nothing was left by her to chance. Matters that seemed trifles to others had an importance for her, because to have them done rightly and arranged properly was a manifestation of harmony, an expression of Principle. Her orderly, methodical life enabled her to get through an amount of business under which most people would have broken down.

The original Church of Christ, Scientist, formed in 1879, had an ordinary charter as a religious corporation of the usual type. The Mother Church, formed in 1892, has an organization in accordance with a Deed of Trust based on a particular Massachusetts statute. It is entitled "The First Church of Christ, Scientist, in Boston, Massachusetts," but while its church buildings are situated in Boston, the Church itself knows no locality, for its membership is drawn from the four corners of the world.

The government of The Mother Church is vested in the Church Manual, which cannot be altered or revised since Mrs. Eddy has passed away, and this Manual is administered, as we have seen, by a Board of Directors. In 1909 she wrote, "I approve the By-laws of The Mother Church, and require the Christian Science Board of Directors to maintain them and sustain them" (Miscellany, pp. 358, 359). The branch churches enjoy the largest local autonomy, whilst held to the central organization by a bond, outwardly slight, though spiritually powerful.

In 1899 Mrs. Eddy wrote of the government of the Church: "Essentially democratic, its government is administered by the common consent of the governed, wherein and whereby man governed by his creator is self-governed. The church is the mouthpiece of Christian Science, — its law and gospel are according to Christ Jesus; its rules are health, holiness, and immortality, — equal rights and privileges, equality of the sexes, rotation in office" (Miscellany, p. 247).

The missionary work of Christian Science is carried on on lines very different from that of the other churches. No attempt is made to mark out any place as a centre for missionary work, and no people are

singled out to act as missionaries, and yet the spread
of Christian Science is admitted to be very surprising,
even by those who are most opposed to its teachings.

In the 16th chapter of the Acts of the Apostles,
we read that St. Paul and his companions thought
of preaching the Gospel in Asia, and shortly afterwards in Bithynia, but that the Holy Ghost "suffered
them not" to carry out these plans. We know that
St. Paul was a man of learning and of experience,
and we cannot doubt that he had what would be
called excellent reasons for thinking those places
ready to receive the Gospel teaching, but it is plain
that his human judgment in this matter was at fault.
As he was constantly looking for the divine guidance,
however, he received timely warning; a spiritual
intuition led him to change his plans, and thus he
was saved from the disappointment and discourage-
ment of a fruitless expedition.

Christian Science teaches that every idea of God
has its right relationship to Mind, and a perception
of this scientific fact improves the dream sense of
things, enabling one to find suitable work in suitable
surroundings. In this attitude, he will find that oppor-
tunities open up for him to tell others about Christian
Science, and to speak of the benefits he has derived
from its study. If the people to whom he mentions
the subject show no interest in it, he leaves them
lovingly alone, knowing no good can be effected
by human pressure and persuasion, however kindly

meant. He does not intrude his views upon them, nor enter into controversy, but remains a kind and considerate neighbour. If, however, they are receptive to the ideas he presents, he rejoices to tell them more, to help them to understand, to free them from fear. They in their turn speak of Christian Science to their friends, their employees or servants; someone is healed by reading the books or by treatment, and a new centre of Christian Science activity has been started. In this way, every student becomes a missionary. Thus this Science has been carried to the remotest parts of the earth, by business men, engineers, civil servants, officers of the navy and army and by men and women of all classes.

We have already heard something about the lecture work. This is also a form of missionary endeavour. Lectures can only be given under the auspices of Churches of Christ, Scientist, societies, and by college organizations. Before a society can be recognized by the Directors of The Mother Church, a good deal of preliminary work must have been done; thus the way has been prepared for the lecture; some interest in Christian Science has been aroused in the place, and there are people really anxious to hear more about it. The object of the lecturer is to give a clear and simple account of some of the leading points of this Science, and to present the facts and testify to the character, life and example of its Discoverer and Founder.

The Reading Room is another Christian Science institution intended primarily for the benefit of the public. Each Church of Christ, Scientist, supports a free Reading Room where in peaceful, comfortable surroundings, anyone may read Mrs. Eddy's books and the periodicals and other literature which emanate from The Christian Science Publishing Society. Here, too, the books can be borrowed or bought, and there is always some one in charge, of whom enquiries may be made. In this way the enquirer can be certain that he is obtaining correct information about Christian Science, instead of being misled by some of the spurious, incorrect, and unauthorized writings on this subject.

The number of Mrs. Eddy's followers had increased so rapidly that by 1902 it was apparent that a much larger building than The Mother Church was required to hold those who wished to attend its services. To relieve the congestion, three branch churches had been formed in the suburbs of Boston in 1899, and later other branch churches were organized in the neighbourhood. Three services, too, were held on Sunday to accommodate the overflowing congregation, and on special occasions, when many Scientists from a distance had come to Boston to attend the Communion Services or the Annual Meeting, it was necessary to engage the largest halls in the city, and yet these were not large enough. At the Annual Meeting in 1902, therefore, the assembled

Christian Scientists pledged themselves and their fellow students to raise any sum up to $2,000,000 that might be required to secure sufficient ground alongside of The Mother Church, and erect on it a building of the necessary size. Four years later the Extension of The Mother Church was dedicated, free of debt, on the 10th of June, 1906. The actual building had occupied nearly two years.

The Extension is a very handsome structure of light grey Bedford stone and New Hampshire granite, with a dome over two hundred and twenty feet high, "forming one of the few perfect sky-lines in an American city," as *The Boston Herald* said. The ground in front, on the opposite side of the roadway, has been bought and laid out in lawns, so that the great church, rising from a carpet of beautiful green turf, is seen to much advantage from the broad thoroughfare of Huntington Avenue.* The Extension seats 5000 people, with remarkable acoustics. It has a fine organ and a beautiful chime of bells.

While she lived in Concord, Mrs. Eddy's influence was felt on the side of progress in the community. The roads were improved, and electric cars superseded the old-fashioned one-horsed 'bus. She gave very generously to city improvements and to many worthy objects. She presented yearly a large gift of boots to the poor children of the place, and con-

---

*Even greater beautification has now come with the completion of the Christian Science Center.

tributed handsomely to various charities, besides sending large contributions to relief funds in distant parts. The church of her childhood was not forgotten, for she helped to repair the North Congregational Church, and though living a very unpretentious and secluded life, came to be regarded as the most distinguished citizen of Concord.

But the animosity which had dogged her steps ever since her discovery of Christian Science, still pursued her. Two well-known American papers made a bitter attack upon her and her friends, in which she was represented as a feeble, decrepit old woman, a prey to superstitious fears, incapable of managing her affairs and controlled by designing persons who were appropriating large sums of her money. Furthermore, it was stated that Mrs. Eddy was no longer able to take her daily drive, but was impersonated by a woman dressed to look like her! These and many other falsehoods were indignantly repudiated by the leading professional and business men of the place, but the relentless persecution went on till it culminated in a suit in equity, ostensibly brought on Mrs. Eddy's behalf by her "Next Friends" — Next of Kin — George W. Glover, one of his daughters, Mrs. Eddy's nephew, George W. Baker, the son of George Sullivan Baker, and Ebenezer J. Foster-Eddy — against the Directors of The Mother Church and six other of Mrs. Eddy's most trusted students and friends.

As the whole matter turned on Mrs. Eddy's mental capacity, it was necessary that she should be interviewed, but out of deference to her, the interview took place at her home, Pleasant View. It was conducted by the three Masters to whom the Judge had entrusted the duty of hearing the evidence and reporting to the Court as to Mrs. Eddy's capacity to manage her affairs intelligently.

She came through this ordeal so well, that it was plain that the plaintiffs would lose their case, so a few days later they withdrew their suit without waiting for the decision to be given against them.

By the advice of her counsel, Mrs. Eddy had arranged to see one of the most distinguished mental specialists in America, and after the collapse of the suit, this Dr. Allan McLane Hamilton made a statement for publication in the *New York Times*. In this statement he declared that Mrs. Eddy was absolutely normal, and possessed of a remarkably clear intellect. He spoke of "the extraordinary intelligence shown in her eyes," which were at times "almost luminous in appearance." "Her whole bearing was dignified and reserved, in perfect accord with what one would expect in a woman of education and refinement." He spoke of her also as taking complete control of all household arrangements, and of the devotion shown her by all who lived with her. "In her ordinary conversation she is witty, a bit satirical, but with a great deal of gentleness in her demeanour to those around her." Her letters, he said, expressed "intellectual good order." She possessed, he said, "continuity of intention and much deliberation," also "capacity to appreciate details."

Dr. Edward French, also a noted mental specialist, had an interview with her the same summer, and said he was impressed with her intelligence and business ability.

In the interview which Dr. Hamilton had with Mrs. Eddy, as well as in the subsequent interview held by the Masters, the subject of investments naturally came up. The interviewers questioned her as to what kind of investments she considered sound. She replied that she preferred government and municipal bonds, and that she had books which she consulted before making an investment in any of the latter. These books gave the population of each of the chief cities, with data as to their valuation, etc., and she said that she only invested her money in cities whose population and wealth appeared to her sufficient to enable them to pay their debts. She had always avoided buying stocks, she said, except in one instance in which she had followed the advice of one of her students, and, in consequence, had lost a large sum of money.

But though Mrs. Eddy was thoroughly competent to manage her business affairs, she had seen in the spring of the year the desirability of freeing herself from these duties. In March, 1907, she appointed three trustees to take entire charge of her property, so that she might be able to devote all her time and attention to matters of greater moment. At about this time she also made a trust deed for the benefit of George W. Glover and his family.

Practically the entire press of America rejoiced at the news of the collapse of the suit. The whole proceedings ran counter to American feeling. The malicious falsehoods which had been spread broadcast, the thinly-veiled attack on a religious denomination, caused general indignation, and great, too, was the indignation expressed at the way in which a woman of advanced age and of the highest character had been harassed and persecuted under the pretence of protecting her and her interests.

Mrs. Eddy's sojourn at Concord was drawing to a close. Pleasant View had long been too small for all the activities which had to be carried on in it, so for that and other important reasons in the following January she removed to a much larger house which stood in grounds of its own at Chestnut Hill, one of the most beautiful suburbs of Boston. Great was the regret of the people of Concord when they found that she was leaving them, and the City Council met and passed resolutions recording this regret, and their appreciation of her beneficence to their city. Mrs. Eddy, too, regretted leaving Concord, and there are many passages in her writings which speak of her affection for the place and its kindly inhabitants.

In the summer after Mrs. Eddy had taken up her abode at Chestnut Hill, an addition to the new Publishing House was in course of construction, to provide for the printing of *The Christian Science Monitor*, the first copy of which appeared on November 25. The great undertaking of starting a daily newspaper occupied much of her time and thought; she also revised the Church Manual and introduced certain changes which she saw would tend to spiritualize the thought of her followers and preserve the simplicity and purity of the Church.

The year 1909 saw her still busy in her work, and in 1910 she was still writing and guiding the affairs of the Church and taking her daily drive as usual up to the end of November. On the first of December, however, she took her last drive. The following day, Friday, she remained in her room, and did not get up on Saturday, and in the evening passed peacefully away without pain or struggle. The last words she wrote were on Thursday afternoon: "God is my life."

"Thou wilt keep him in perfect peace, whose mind is stayed on thee." Outwardly, Mrs. Eddy's life had been one of almost constant struggle, but her faith in God's goodness had never faltered, and she had been wonderfully supported in all the trials and difficulties which had beset her path. When she passed away in her ninetieth year, she had the happiness of knowing that Christian Science was firmly established.

Her opponents had often declared that the whole system rested on Mrs. Eddy's personality, and that with her death it would fall to pieces, but many years have passed and the movement is constantly gaining in strength and in numbers.

WHAT HAS MARY BAKER EDDY DONE
FOR THE WORLD?

SHE has furnished us with a key by which we may enter into the heart of the Gospel teaching. She has cleared away the ignorance and superstition which through long centuries have hung about the words and works of our Lord. She has shown us that Christianity contains and acknowledges no mysteries, but declares that there is nothing in God's universe which man may not know, since he is made in the image and likeness of infinite Mind. She has proved to us by actual demonstration that the Master's words are statements of scientific truth, his commands possible of fulfillment by the men and women of to-day, his works the visible manifestation of unchanging law. In this way she has shown Christianity to be logical, complete in every part, and has thereby satisfied men's reasoning powers and given them a sure foundation for their faith.

Christian Science appears to its students as by far the most outstanding discovery of this age. It has brought deliverance to an immense number of sufferers, has healed every form of disease, hereditary and organic, and has performed many well-attested cases of mental surgery. It has made known the laws of thought, enabling us to distinguish between true thought and false; it has shown us the irresistible power of right thought — the activity of the Mind which is God — the impotence of wrong thought when understood as without cause and confronted by the true. It has shown us the nearness of the things of Spirit, the availability of God; it is leading us constantly to look to Him for guidance and help in all the affairs of everyday life, in our studies, our business, in all that concerns our private or public life, from the smallest affairs of the home to questions that affect the welfare of the world at large. Christian Science has shown us the nature of the Principle of the universe, and so given us a standard of right. It has shown why one cannot gain at the expense of another, either as an individual or as a state, and as we become conscious of the government of Principle, even in a very slight degree, this brings with it a sense of poise and security unknown to us before.

As Christian Science satisfies our intelligence and reason, so, too, it satisfies the heart. It opens the door of expectation and receptivity, and brings us into touch with the inexpressible tenderness of the divine Mind. Few, indeed, are there of the sons of men who do not suffer from some sense of loneliness, injustice, neglect, disappointment, unsatisfied yearning, though they may hide these feelings from their fellow men, and may hardly admit them to themselves; but this practical living consciousness of God's nearness, of His infinite care, of the beauty and radiance of His love, embracing, supporting, with more than a mother's tenderness or a father's strength, makes the waste places of the heart to blossom as the rose.

Mrs. Eddy's teachings have revealed to us spiritual realms of which we had known nothing, capacities and possibilities for good of which we had never dreamed. To launch our boats out into the shining waters of these unknown seas is the greatest adventure of the ages; it requires courage, perseverance, all the heroic qualities, and yet it is only through humility, purity, unselfish obedience to Principle, to God's law, that anything can be accomplished.

Once an individual begins to recognize himself as an idea of God, and is willing to put off his personal self with its pride and fear and weakness, he finds that the joy and enthusiasm of youth, the steadfastness and wisdom of riper years, the beautiful qualities manifested by men and by women are expressions of God's nature, and therefore ever present and to be reflected by all. Thus he begins to enter into his heritage of completeness.

To establish this teaching, Mary Baker Eddy devoted to it forty years of unremitting toil, and, whenever assailed or opposed, she consistently returned good for evil and always retained her dignity and serenity as well as her love for God and man.

Index

Christian Science and Its Discoverer

8-543210 7-987
0987654321